SHEBOYGAN
TALES OF THE
TRAGIC & BIZARRE

SHEBOYGAN

TALES OF THE TRAGIC & BIZARRE

WILLIAM WANGEMANN

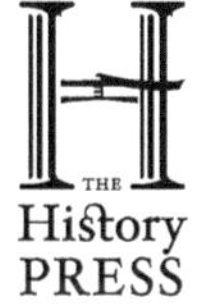

Published by The History Press
Charleston, SC 29403
www.historypress.net

Front cover: Painting of ship by William F. Wangemann.
First published 2010

ISBN 978.1.5402.0503.2

Library of Congress Cataloging-in-Publication Data
Wangemann, William.
Sheboygan tales of the tragic and bizarre / William Wangemann.
p. cm.
ISBN 978-1-60949-035-5
1. Sheboygan County (Wis.)--History--Anecdotes. 2. Sheboygan County (Wis.)--History, Local--Anecdotes. 3. Tragedy--Social aspects--Wisconsin--Sheboygan County--History--Anecdotes. 4. Death--Wisconsin--Sheboygan County--History--Anecdotes. 5. Curiosities and wonders--Wisconsin--Sheboygan County--Anecdotes. 6. Sheboygan County (Wis.)--Biography--Anecdotes. I. Title.
F587.S5W36 2010
977.5'69--dc22
2010032878

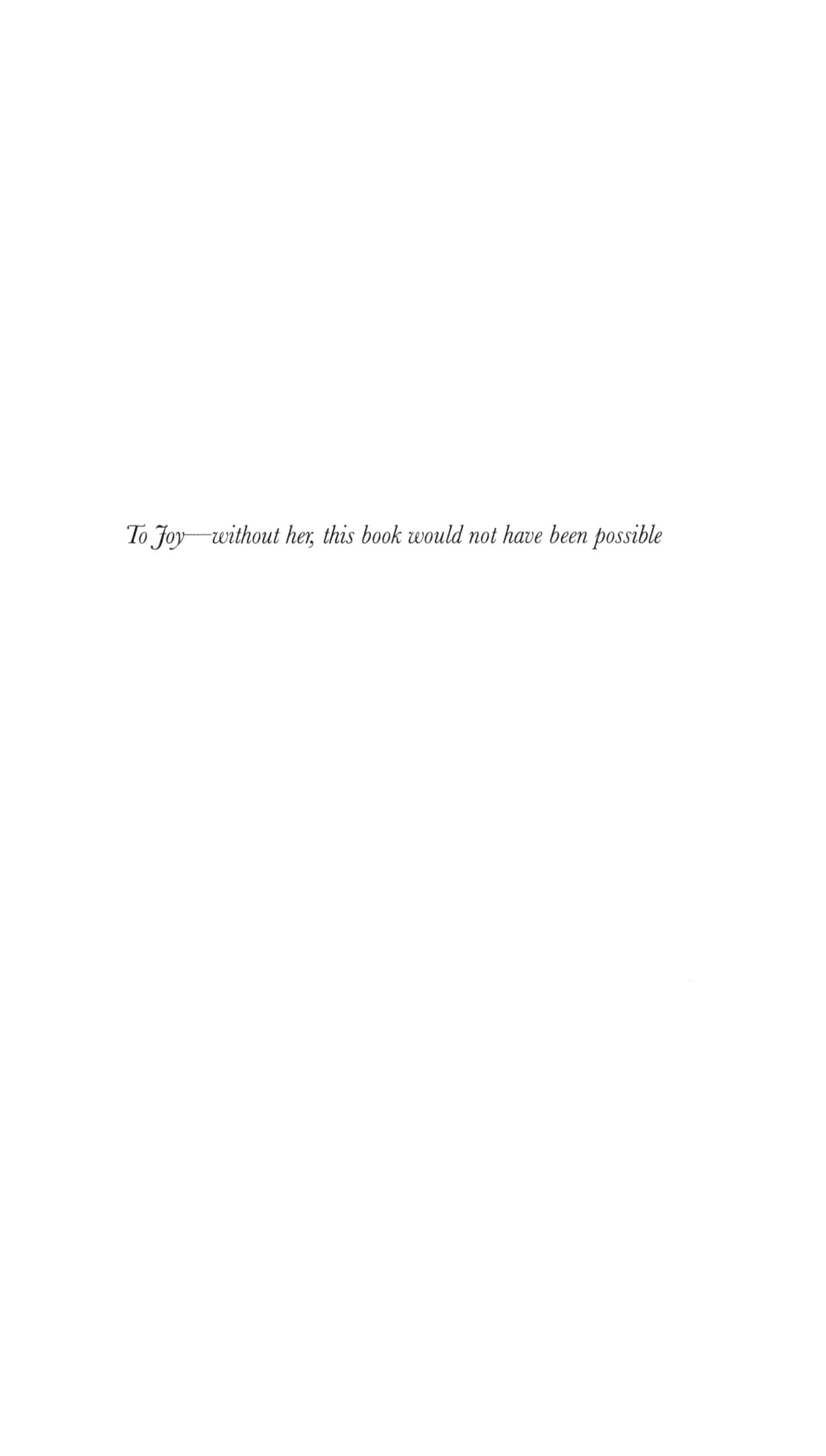

To Joy—without her, this book would not have been possible

CONTENTS

Contents

PREFACE

To clarify things, I'm neither a professional writer nor a professional historian. Two facts that had a direct effect on the stories told in this book are: I have lived on the shores of Lake Michigan all my life, and for twenty-eight years I was a professional police officer. Most of the information relating to the stories comes from local newspapers, old court records, some from personal experiences and others from interviews with old-timers. A good number of the photographs came from my own collection and the files of the Sheboygan County Historic Research Center. I'd like to pay a special tribute to Ed Sofa, a highly talented artist, for the wonderful pen-and-ink drawings in this book. Ed, who I considered a friend, passed away much too young. A very special thanks to Beth and Cathy for all their invaluable help in assembling the pictures for this book.

CHAPTER 1
TRAGIC TALES

A Flaming End to a Voyage of Dreams

The litany of disasters on the Great Lakes goes back to prehistoric times when ancient man first used the waters of the turbulent inland seas for travel. In Indian lore, it's recorded that on several occasions disasters struck without warning to these early lake sailors. On a date lost in time, nearly the entire male population of one tribe was wiped out during a lake voyage. The lost tribe set out in canoes from the tip of Door County bound for Washington Island, a mere five miles away, to attack a tribe they were at war with. A sudden gale that the Great Lakes are so well known for struck without warning. When the storm subsided, the entire male population of the attacking tribesmen was lost. The strait between the tip of Door County and Washington Island was then known by French fur trappers as La Porte de Morts, or the Door of Death, from which Door County got its name.

When the Dutch immigrants at last reached the Great Lakes, they were awed and stunned by the sheer size of the freshwater giants that lay before them. The Great Lakes are truly one of the great wonders of the world. With America's longest shoreline, at over 10,000 miles, and containing 5,412 cubic miles of water, these vast inland oceans were difficult for the newcomers to comprehend.

Standing on the shore of any one of Great Lakes during a warm July afternoon and looking out across its placid blue waters, one could easily be led to believe that the lakes pose no threat. It is the Great Lakes' history itself that is mute testimony to the fact that these gentle giants can turn into raging

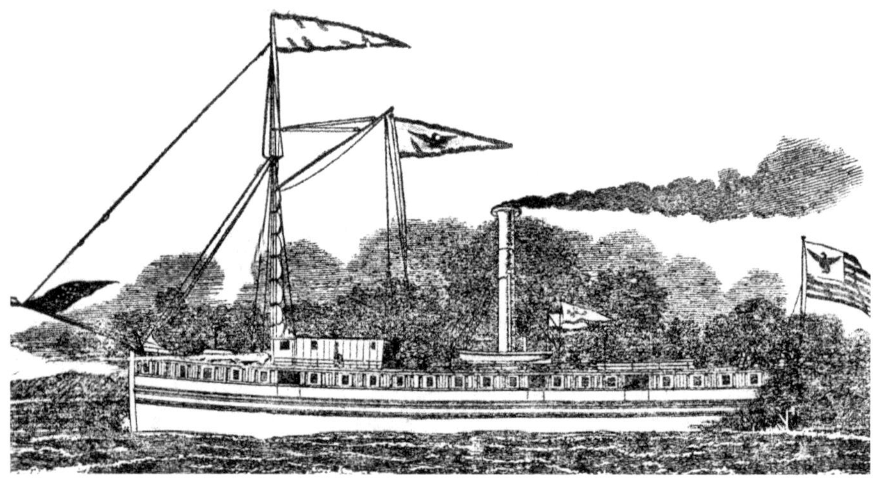

A sketch of the steamer *Phoenix* from an old advertising poster. *Courtesy Sheboygan County Historic Research Center.*

demons with no warning. But weather is not the only threat encountered by any who dare challenge these freshwater behemoths. In the winter there is ice, and in all months thick blankets of fog, with its ever-present threat of collision, still take their toll. In the time of the *Phoenix*, as well as today, the most dreaded calamity that can befall a vessel is fire.

In the year 1847, waves of turmoil swept across Holland as a religious reform movement gained momentum. Those who embraced this new form of their staid old religion were looked down upon and shunned. Ticket agents for shipping companies traveled the length and breadth of Holland capitalizing on the unrest by extolling the great promise offered to those who had the courage to immigrate to America. The agents, who worked on commission, told enticing tales of vast areas of fertile land selling for as little as $1.25 per acre. They talked of plentiful rainfall, short, warm winters and an endless supply of cheap lumber obtained from immeasurable forests. The ticket hawkers painted a picture of the new territories, in what was to become Wisconsin, as a virtual land of milk and honey.

The story of the *Phoenix* is one of hopes held high for a new life of freedom in a new world. All too tragically, these dreams came to a fiery end. For over three hundred immigrants after a 3,700-mile journey and just 7 heartbreaking miles short of their destination, their dreams ended. It is also the story of bravery above and beyond human endurance and the savage law of self-preservation, not altogether unlike the sinking of the *Titanic*.

On November 21, 1847, at about 2:00 a.m. just a few miles north of Sheboygan, one of the most dreadful and poignant disasters in the history of the Great Lakes occurred. The propeller steamer *Phoenix* carried a complement of over 350 persons, including passengers and crew. When it suddenly burst into flames, fewer than 50 people survived. Most of those lost were Dutch immigrants who had sailed on August 26, 1847, from Rotterdam, Holland, on board an oceangoing sailing ship. After an uncomfortable crossing of sixty-one days, the immigrants at last arrived in New York on October 26, 1847.

The water-weary travelers were anxious to get their feet back on dry land, but this was not to be. As their ship slowly entered the crowded harbor, it dropped its anchor far from any pier where the immigrants might disembark. The puzzled passengers were informed that first a doctor would come on board to certify that they carried no communicable diseases. Furthermore, personal information had to be gathered from each newcomer by immigration officials. Disappointed, the weary people sat down to wait. All around them, ships lay at anchor; the harbor was a virtual forest of masts. At last, after a wait of several hours, a small sloop was seen putting out from shore and began heading for their ship. Soon the sloop drew alongside the immigrants' ship, and several very official-looking men boarded. As promised, one of the men was a doctor and the other was an immigration official. After quickly examining the passengers, the doctor declared the ship was disease free and cleared them to land—but only after the immigration representative gathered the pertinent information needed to allow foreigners to enter the United States.

Before he left the ship, the customs agent, through an interpreter, warned the people not to go ashore unless absolutely necessary. The agent went on to explain that the waterfront was plagued with numerous vicious gangs looking for immigrants to rob. Knowing that many of them carried large sums of cash to fund their new lives in America, the cruel predators found the immigrants to be easy prey. The customs agent further stated that if they were accosted by these evil bandits and they even slightly resisted, the thieves would not hesitate to kill them.

After learning that most of the travelers were headed to the Wisconsin territories and planned to take a riverboat up the Hudson River to Albany and then on the Erie Canal to the Great Lakes, the official strongly suggested they take a small sailing boat to where the riverboat was docked. After a quick conference among the Dutchmen, it was decided that a trip by water to the riverboat was the most prudent.

The boat then moved to a pier, where a few of the passengers disembarked. Not long after the immigration agent left, a representative of the Netherland Society for the Protection of Emigrants from Holland came aboard to assist the Dutch people. Arrangements were made to transfer to the riverboat for the trip up the Hudson River to Albany. The agent also arranged the fare for their passage on the canalboats of the Erie Canal.

Once on board the side-wheel steamer, the immigrants found that their daylong trip to Albany was quite pleasant. They arrived at Albany, and upon boarding the canalboats, the Hollanders discovered that pleasant was not a word that could be used to describe this portion of their trip. The canalboats (the Hollanders needed three of them) were overcrowded and dirty. The fare of one and a half cents per mile included food, if you could call it that. The quality was poor, and food was badly cooked. Sleeping accommodations were only slightly better. The interior of the boat where the sleeping quarters were located consisted of one long room with crude bunks built along the sides. As there were not nearly enough bunks for everyone, many had to sleep on the floor. It became quite clear from early on that the trip on the Erie Canal was going to be no picnic. After one very long week, the travelers at last reached Buffalo, New York, where they were to board a lake steamer that was to take them on the final leg of their seemingly endless trip.

Buffalo then, as it is now, was the gateway to the Great Lakes. When the Dutchmen arrived in Buffalo, they found the city jammed with immigrants from practically every European nation. It was said that if you stood on a street corner on the waterfront long enough, you could hear every European language spoken. Many of the newcomers were still wearing clothing representative of their native countries. With bewildered looks on their faces and clutching bundles of their belongings, they plainly stood out from the local population. But much to the relief of the immigrants, unlike in New York, there was no thievery or danger to those waiting to board boats.

Before leaving New York, the Dutch immigrants were given the name and address of a Dutch-speaking pastor in Buffalo who it was said would help them book passage on a lake steamer. The pastor was located, and he booked passage on the same steamer for the entire group, which numbered some 250 persons. The immigrants were delighted to learn that the boat they were booked on was the three-year-old, modern steamboat, the *Phoenix*. It would not be long before their delight would turn to horror.

It was getting late in November, and a great rush was on to get the boats in the harbor underway before winter came upon them and turned the lakes into an impenetrable mass of ice. Most captains refused to sail after

November 1, as the gales of November were notorious and deeply feared by lake mariners. They knew only too well that more boats were lost to storms in November than any other month. In fact, insurance companies refused to insure boats after November 1. The lure of making one more run, even without insurance, and the profit that could be made in the lucrative business of transporting immigrants was too much to resist for some boat owners. So it was with Pease and Allen Shipping Company, the owners of one of the finest boats on the Great Lakes, the three-year-old propeller steamer *Phoenix*. The owners of the *Phoenix* took great pride, and rightfully so, in their new boat, which was on the cutting edge of the technology of the day. Only three years before, the very first propeller-driven steamboat, the *Vandalia*, had appeared on the Great Lakes. Prior to this, all steamboats on the lakes had been driven by bulky side-mounted paddle wheels. The fragile paddle wheels, while being efficient, were very prone to damage in storms, collisions and docking accidents. The *Phoenix* was a very special propeller (as they were called), for it sported a completely revolutionary twin propeller system. The twin propellers were driven by one shaft that ran to a gearbox, and then two shafts exited the gear box and drove both propellers. The propellers looked nothing like a modern-day propeller. This wonder of engineering looked

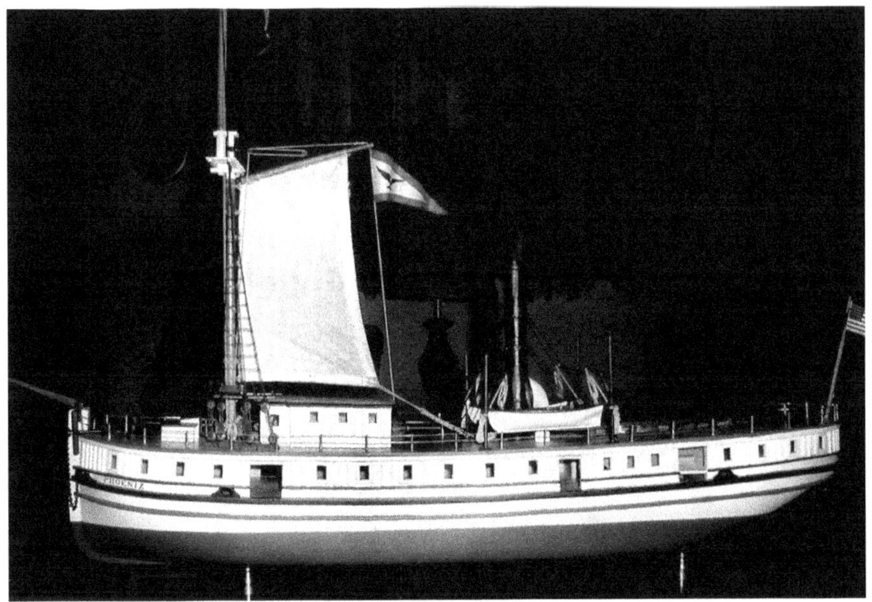

A scale model of the *Phoenix* with its sail raised. *Model built by Captain Rocky Groh; photo by the author.*

like a barrel with a band of metal fastened to its exterior in the fashion of a corkscrew. The twin propellers were then connected to the two drive shafts that propelled the boat. This wonder of marine technology was invented by none other than John Erickson. It may be remembered that in later years, John Erickson designed and built an ironclad war ship for the Union navy during the Civil War, named the *Monitor*.

At last, the last bit of cargo was loaded and the final passenger had boarded. The date was November 11, 1847, and it was time for the *Phoenix* to cast off for its last run of the season. It was, in fact, its last run for any season. Its cargo of hardware, chains, coffee and molasses had been stowed safely away. The passengers, numbering about 350, of which 70 were American citizens, had all boarded and stowed their bags and baggage. The first-class passengers were assigned cabins that occupied the forward part of the boat, while the immigrants were consigned to the after portions of the vessel. The first-class passengers settled into what, for the day, were considered spacious quarters. The immigrants, carrying their ponderous bundles and bags of belongings, found themselves crowded into one long room that was to be

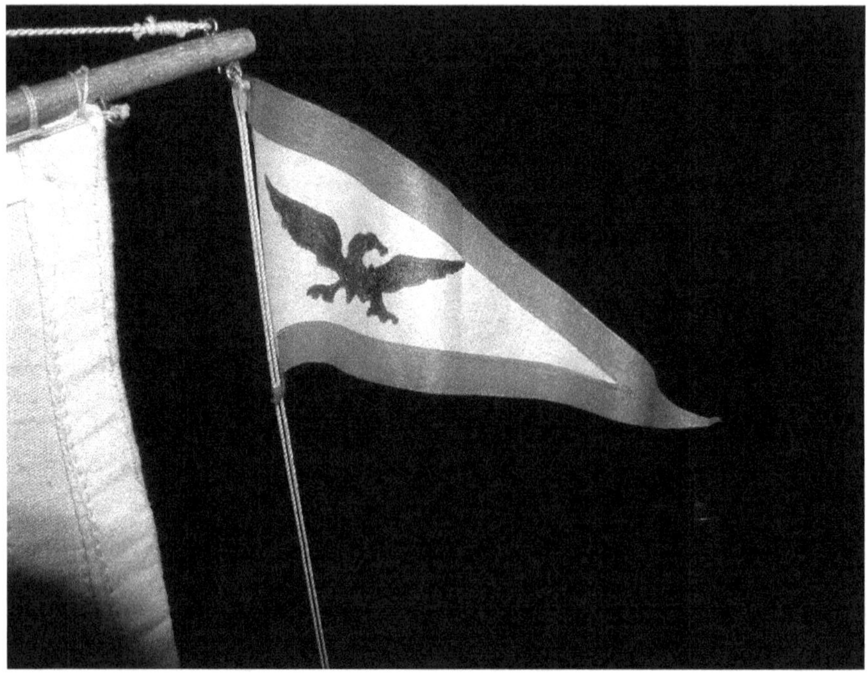

The *Phoenix* flag depicting the immortal phoenix bird. *Courtesy Captain Groh.*

their home for the next ten days. In the very center of the boat could be found the engine room with its large hissing and clanking steam engine and the roaring boiler that generated the steam needed to propel the boat. To say that to place a red-hot boiler in an all-wooden boat painted with flammable oil paints and varnishes is inviting disaster would today be a gross understatement of the potential for a flaming holocaust.

The *Phoenix*, at 140 feet, 6 inches long with a breadth of 22 feet, 7 inches, was considered a large boat for the day. Its rolled iron smokestack towered over 26 feet above its deck. Toward the forward part of the boat, it had a tall mast that was capable of carrying sail, if the steam engines should fail. All early steamboats still carried mast and sail in those days. Even though the changeover from sail to steam was rapidly taking place, there was a certain amount of distrust of the clanking, hissing beasts that drove their boats forward. Most captains still wanted the tried and true sail available—just in case.

As for safety equipment, the *Phoenix* was equipped with the finest state-of-the-art, high-pressure, steam-driven water pumps and the very best linen fire hoses available. This modern firefighting equipment had already been put to the test. During its maiden voyage, a small fire was detected in the boiler room. Coincidentally, the list of passengers for what was to be a festive occasion included most of the members of the Buffalo Fire Department, who, when the fire was discovered, quickly sprang into action and, utilizing the new firefighting equipment, put out the fire.

Sailors in those days were a superstitious lot and considered a fire during a boat's trial run a very dark omen of things to come. They could not have imagined how right they were. Tragically, the lifeboats were woefully inadequate, a fact that in just a few days would become all too clear. The lifeboats, each of which could hold thirty or forty persons at the most, were slung from davits near the center of the boat. Some have said that the boat carried three lifeboats, with the third one slung from davits at the stern of the boat, but early drawings of the *Phoenix* do not indicate this. Even though photography had already been invented, it was still in its infancy, and no known photo of the *Phoenix* exists.

The Pease and Allen Shipping Company, owners of the *Phoenix*, had exercised great care in the selection of a captain for their new boat. After much thought, they selected Captain G.B. Sweet to be placed in command. Along with First Officer Mr. Watts, the company felt they had two of the best and most experienced sailors on the Great Lakes.

The boat was ready, the cold winds of mid-November were blowing and it was time to get underway. Captain Sweet was very familiar with the evil

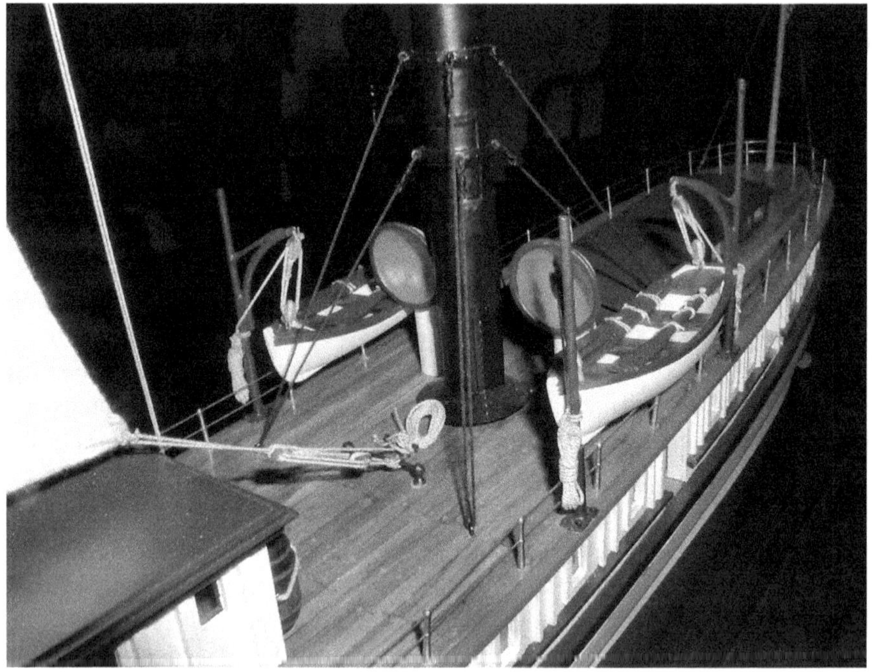

The only two lifeboats on the *Phoenix*. *Courtesy Captain Groh.*

temperament of the Great Lakes and was anxious to complete his round-trip voyage to Chicago and back, a trip that took nearly three weeks. The boiler room signaled that they were carrying a full head of steam; dockhands were ordered to cast off all lines. The order was given to the engine room for slow astern, and the *Phoenix* backed away from the dock. When clear of the dock, the engines were reversed and began to move the ill-fated boat forward. As the *Phoenix* picked up speed, it headed out into Lake Erie, and it, its passengers and crew sailed into history.

As the *Phoenix* sailed out into the turbulent lake, some of the passengers lined the rail and watched the distant shoreline splashed with late autumn colors of red, gold and every shade of brown disappear. Overhead, long Vs of geese noisily winged their way south. Soon the last trace of the shoreline dipped below the horizon. They were now surrounded by what seemed to be a boiling caldron of surging blue waves, each one bigger than the last. The immigrants on the storm-lashed deck soon scurried for cover.

At times the bow of the *Phoenix* was completely submerged by the blue green rollers, only in the next moment to suddenly rise with its bow pointing to the sky. And so it went; hour after hour the boat was battered by the remorseless waves. During this time, Captain Sweet, who was getting on in years, lost his balance and was thrown heavily to the deck. Historical accounts differ as to what injury he suffered, but what is known is that Captain Sweet was seriously injured, unable to walk, and was carried to his cabin. On the captain's orders, Mr. Watts took command of the *Phoenix*.

Even though the sturdy little steamer was taking a battering, it made steady progress forward. The *Phoenix* had been built by skilled hands and was able handle the storm, but the passengers could not. In the steerage-class quarters, chaos reigned supreme. Everywhere seasick men, women and children slid back and forth across the deck made slippery by vomit. Overturned buckets, which had been used as commodes, all mingled in with the scattered belongings. To add to the immigrants' discomfort, windows in their sparse quarters were smashed in by marauding torrents of icy lake water.

As the little steamer headed west on Lake Erie, they were in the vicinity of Long Point, which juts out into Lake Erie and is a traditional shelter for storm-tossed ships. The first mate considered sheltering behind the point until the waters calmed. A hasty conference was held with the injured captain in his quarters, and it was decided that the *Phoenix* was suffering no serious difficulties and should continue on its course. The decision proved to be a wise one, as the waves began to moderate and the winds died down. At last, the battered little vessel reached the St. Mary's River, which is the connecting waterway to Lake Huron. The trip on the St. Mary's River was, for the Hollanders, a welcome respite from the torturing storms. The Dutch, a traditionally fastidious people, immediately began to clean and scour their quarters. The *Phoenix* then passed the bustling and fast-growing city of Detroit and entered Lake St. Clair. After a quiet passage across the calm waters of Lake St. Clair, the *Phoenix* again entered the St. Mary's River and headed toward Lake Huron. Immigrants hoped and prayed that the rest of their voyage would find the waters of the Great Lakes in a calmer mood. This prayer was not granted.

Lake Huron was in no better mood than its agitated sister, Lake Erie. The *Phoenix*, which was now headed north up Lake Huron, was again pummeled by the unmerciful waves of an angry lake. After several days of very difficult travel, they at last arrived at the northern end of Lake Huron, turned into the Straits of Mackinac and passed into Lake Michigan, and still the storms raged. It was decided, by the injured captain from his sickbed, that the boat, its passengers and crew could take no more, and he ordered the *Phoenix* to take refuge from the storm behind Beaver Island, located at the far northern end of Lake Michigan.

For several days, the weary passengers and crew tried to repair the damage done by the endless storms. After several days, the water seemed to calm and the wind abated. Upon entering Lake Michigan, the normal course for the *Phoenix* would be down the western side of Lake Michigan to its first port of call, the tiny frontier village of Sheboygan. On this voyage, the *Phoenix*, carrying cargo and passengers, was bound for Manitowoc. With the weather moderating, the *Phoenix* hastily departed Beaver Island and set a course for Manitowoc. Unbelievably, the waves rose once again to try and bar their way. Finally, the pier head at Manitowoc came into sight, and the *Phoenix* gratefully sailed into the Manitowoc harbor. Several passengers disembarked, the cargo consigned to Manitowoc was unloaded and once again the decision was made to wait for the lake to calm. The date was November 20, 1847.

While the crew of the *Phoenix* waited for calmer weather, they requested permission from the captain to go ashore and seek those pleasures that for thousands of years water-weary sailors have always sought. However, before the crew men left, they were given strict orders to return to the ship at once if they heard the *Phoenix* sound its whistle. At approximately midnight, the skies cleared and the winds dropped to zero. It was immediately decided that they would depart as soon as the crew returned. After a long blast on the ships steam whistle, the crew came scurrying back. Later, some passengers claimed that many of the crew men were greatly intoxicated.

The *Phoenix* made all preparations to get underway at once. Three dock workers cast off the mooring lines. As they stood watching the lights of the ship disappear out on the dark lake, little did they realize that they would be the last people on shore to see it afloat. It was now November 21, 1847, approximately 2:00 a.m., a day the survivors of the *Phoenix* would never forget.

The weather was absolutely calm; the surface of the lake was as shiny and smooth as a piece of black glass. Overhead in a moonless but clear sky, millions of stars sparkled like diamonds from horizon to horizon. Each glittering star reproduced itself as a twinkling reflection on the surface of the icy water. It seemed that at long last the gales of November were over. A few men were standing at the rail gazing skyward, enthralled by the beauty of the night. The *Phoenix*, now under a full head of steam, was racing through the night at top speed; a white wake curled back from its bow and disappeared into the night in an ever-widening V. A crew member mentioned to several of the Hollanders that Sheboygan, their destination, was less than thirty miles away. At first they did not react, and then suddenly it occurred to them that after many long months, weeks and days their endless journey was almost over! They peered through the night toward the dark shore, trying to catch a glimpse of their destination. Suddenly one of them cried out, "There, I saw a light!" Soon the others saw it as well; it had to be Sheboygan. The men rushed into the immigrant quarters and began waking people up. Soon a great wave of excitement swept through their group.

The news that at last the long journey was nearly over caused a great deal of commotion on board the *Phoenix*, resulting in some of the first-class passengers being awakened. One of them was an Irishman, traveling with his wife and daughter, who it is believed was named O'Conner. In Ireland, O'Conner had been the operator of a large stationary steam engine in a factory. Before the advent of electric motors, many factories used steam power to run all the machines in the factory through a system of shafts and belts. Unable to get back to sleep, the Irishman lay in his bunk listening to the steady throb of the ship's engines, but to his trained ear something sounded wrong. Normally, the engines had a smooth, rhythmic sound, but tonight they were emitting a loud, clanking noise and seemed to be running rough. To O'Conner, this meant only one thing: the engines were low on water. O'Conner quickly jumped out of bed, dressed and hurried to the engine room. Steam engines that become low on water can severely overheat and present a great fire hazard. As he opened the engine room door, O'Conner was struck by a sudden blast of heat and noise. The third engineer was on duty at the time and looked up in surprise when he came in, as passengers are never allowed in the engine room. The third engineer immediately ordered the Irishman out. When O'Conner tried to explain to the engineer that he thought the engines were overheating, the third engineer became furious. First the upstart Irishman invaded his engine room, and then he was telling him how to operate his engine; this was too much to bear. The engineer planted a stout blow to O'Conner's jaw, knocking him down; he was then thrown bodily out of the engine room.

Convinced that he was right, O'Conner rushed back to his cabin and awakened his wife and daughter. He told them to dress quickly in their warmest cloths and come with him, as he was sure the ship was going to catch fire. Once his family was dressed, he escorted them out onto the deck and to one of the two lifeboats the *Phoenix* carried. O'Conner then pulled the canvas cover off and helped his wife and daughter into the boat. He told them that he was going to return to their cabin for a few personal possessions, and under no circumstances were they to leave the boat, as the ship was about to catch fire. They did not have long to wait. It seemed that the Irishman had barely left his family when the dreaded cry "Fire!" rang out. The time was about 2:00 a.m. on November 21, 1847.

At first, the Hollanders on deck did not grasp what was happening. They watched in wonder as crew members rushed about the decks and began pulling out fire hoses. But soon it became all too apparent, as the windows of the engine room lit up with flickering, dancing tongues of flame. Suddenly, the heat blew out several engine room windows, and shafts of flame shot out of the windows and arched skyward. Panic ensued. Then the engine room crew staggered onto to the deck, their faces blackened. Coughing and gasping for air, they sunk to the deck. They had abandoned the engine room.

The captain was notified and immediately ordered the boat be turned toward the shore, now but a mile away, in an attempt to beach it. The rationale behind that order was that if the ship was beached and the passengers and crew had to abandon ship, it would be easier for them to reach the safety of land. The helmsmen put the wheel hard over, steered for the shore and called for maximum speed; there was no answer from the engine room, as the place had become a roaring inferno. With no one to feed the ever-hungry boilers, the fires in the boilers died down, steam pressure dropped and the ship slowed and then stopped. One of the many bitter ironies of the *Phoenix* was that while fire raged throughout the ship, the only place they needed fire was in the boilers, and there they had none. The dropping steam pressure also caused the pumps supplying water to the fire hoses to slow, sputter and then quit. The *Phoenix* was doomed.

A young businessman named David Blish, from Southport, now known as Kenosha, was asleep in his first-class cabin when he was awakened by the chaos now taking place on deck. Blish dressed, ran out of his cabin and was appalled by the horrific scene before him. The ship lay dead in the water. The engine room was completely engulfed in flames, which had also spread to the quarters of the immigrants. People were rushing about the deck in terror not knowing what to do; their only option was to abandon ship.

Much as on the *Titanic*, the first-class passengers were given first chance at a seat in one of the two lifeboats. Captain Sweet was carried from his cabin and protested loudly as he was placed in a boat, as he felt it was his duty to stay with his ship. Mr. Blish refused a seat in the lifeboat, saying he preferred to stay with the Hollanders, many of whom he had made friends with. The boats were lowered, pulled away from the stricken ship and headed for shore about a mile away. There were still 250 to 300 persons on board the *Phoenix*.

Many of those still on board felt that surely the boats would return. They did not. By now, many immigrants were faced with the terrible choice of burning to death or jumping into icy Lake Michigan. Fearing the flames more than the water, most jumped. The water in Lake Michigan in late November hovers around forty degrees. To survive in the frigid water for more than thirty minutes is nearly impossible.

As the lifeboats pulled away from the ship, they passed through a sea of bobbing heads. Frantic hands reached out and tried to grasp the gunwales of the boats as they passed. Pitiful screams for help and prayers went unanswered. It was now that the savage law of self-preservation reared its ugly heard. As people near drowning tried to cling to the lifeboats, they were pushed back and fingers were pried loose. Others were beaten back with oars, fearful that those in the water might capsize the boat. People who only hours before were friends, neighbors or maybe even relatives were sent to a certain death.

Meanwhile, on board the flaming ship, David Blish did all he could to assist the terrified Hollanders, many of whom he considered to be his friends. He organized a bucket brigade; soon he realized that this was a futile effort. Then the heroic Blish encouraged men to throw anything into the water that might support life. Husky young farmers began tearing doors off their hinges and throwing them and furniture over the side, along with crates and boxes or whatever else they could find that would float.

Tragic scenes followed. Two young sisters, the Hazeltons of Sheboygan, daughters of the owner of the popular Merchants Hotel, were returning from an eastern boarding school. The young girls had become deeply homesick and begged their father to allow them to return home. At last their father, who wanted them to have an excellent education, relented and sent them the money to come back to Sheboygan. Driven from their cabin, the girls found themselves nearly surrounded by searing flames. Little by little, the flames drove the two frightened girls toward the back of the ship. They retreated back farther and farther until they were trapped in the stern. When last seen, the girls had climbed over the rail, and with their arms wrapped around one another, they jumped into the dark frigid water. They disappeared immediately.

Several young men, in a hopeless attempt to escape the flames, climbed the ship's mast. The stays supporting the mast were heavily tarred ropes that soon caught fire. In horror, the occupants of the mast watched as one by one the stays burned through. As the last stay parted, the mast teetered and then fell toward the stern, casting its occupants into the inferno below.

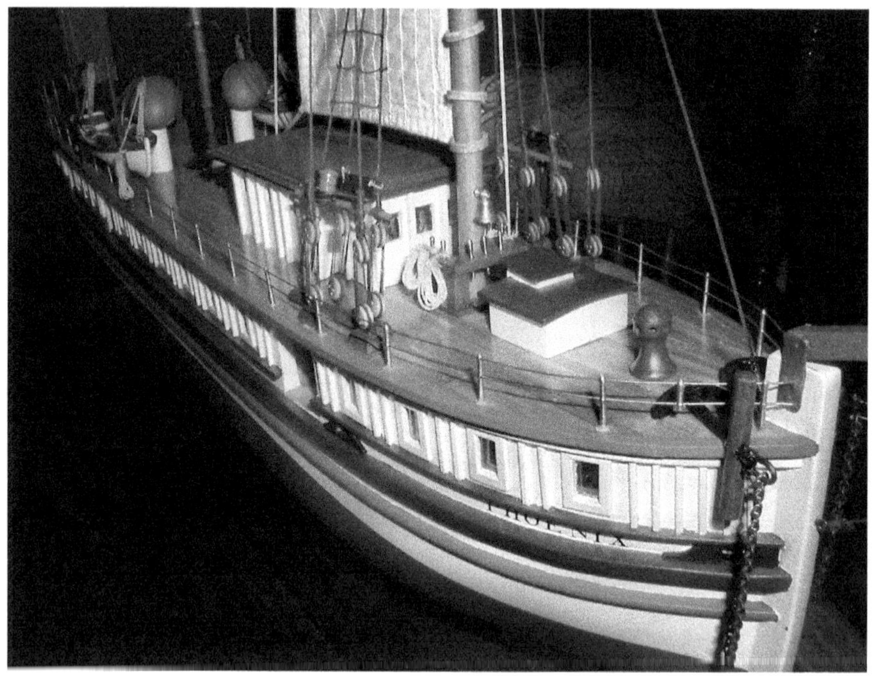

Several frantic young men tried to climb the mast in the fore part of the ship to escape the flames. *Courtesy Captain Groh.*

No more than seven or eight miles to the south, the immigrants' final destination, Sheboygan, lay slumbering under the cold autumn sky. The tiny frontier village was blissfully unaware of the disaster taking place just off its shores. On a high bluff overlooking Lake Michigan, Judge Morris, who was asleep in his fine home, stirred in his sleep. The judge awakened, sat up in bed and looked around the room trying to figure out what it was that had disturbed his sleep. The sleepy man, still trying to brush the drug of sleep from his eyes, slipped out of bed, walked to a nearby dresser and picked up his big gold pocket watch. The time was 2:45 a.m. Looking out a nearby window, the judge saw a large red glow in the sky over the lake. His first thought was that it was the sun coming up. Then suddenly he realized that the sun does not rise at 2:45 a.m. in November! Taking a closer look, the judge noted that what he saw was not a steady glow but a lurid flickering and dancing glow, which could mean only one thing: a ship was in terrible trouble. As quickly as he could, Judge Morris pulled his clothing on over his nightshirt. Running down the steps of his darkened home, he hurriedly pulled on an overcoat and rushed to the harbor.

Sheboygan's harbor was a great deal different in those days than it is now. Due to a sandbar that continually formed at the mouth of the Sheboygan River, ships could not enter the river. The shoreline we know today is about eight or nine hundred feet east of the shoreline of 1847. A large wooden pier, over one thousand feet long, jutted out into Lake Michigan from Center Avenue, which provided a place for ships visiting Sheboygan to tie up and unload or take on passengers. The pier was still under construction, with the end farthest from the beach consisting of only pilings driven into the lake bottom. The planking that was to form the floor of the pier had not yet been installed. It was here, at this unfinished end, that the *Phoenix* would find its final resting place.

The judge rushed to the harbor and found the schooner *Liberty* and the small steamer *Delaware*. Rushing on board the *Delaware*, he began pounding on doors. Hearing the disturbance on deck, Captain Tuttle, the master of the *Delaware*, leapt out of bed and, still in his nightshirt, grabbed his shotgun and rushed on deck to investigate. As soon as the captain came on deck, he saw the flames in the sky to the north and immediately realized that a ship was on fire and needed help. But the *Delaware* could not move, as its boilers were cold. The ship's engineer was rousted from his bed and ordered to light off the boilers at once. The boiler room crew was ordered to get underway as soon as there was enough steam to turn the engines over. The commotion on board the *Delaware* also woke the crew of the nearby *Liberty*, but due to the calm night it could not move either. No one had to tell Captain Porter of the *Liberty* to mount a rescue operation; the flames in the sky said it all. The schooner crew quickly lowered a boat and set out toward the ugly red smear in the sky. Six pairs of strong arms pulled toward the stricken ship. On board the *Delaware*, every eye in the boiler room was glued to the steam gauge. Sweating crew men stuffed four foot lengths of sweet-smelling pine into the roaring fire. The steam gauge gave a wiggle and then bounced a few times, and at last it began to rise. A soon as it had enough steam to move, the little side-wheeler cast off its lines and got underway.

The flames, by this time, had consumed most of the upper works of the *Phoenix*. Only a small portion of the forward structure still stood. In some places, the ship had burned nearly to the water line. A red glow surrounded the ship from the fires still smoldering deep in the hull. Everything was quiet now; no longer could anguished cries for help or pleading prayers be heard. The frightened small voices of children, crying out for their parents from whom they had been separated, were now quiet. The *Phoenix* was a dead ship; it floated aimlessly on a dead calm lake. Most of the passengers were dead, as well as many of the crew. The glassy surface of the lake was littered with debris and floating victims, many very small. The icy fingers of Lake Michigan had claimed them all. With the victims went their hopes and dreams for a better life in a new world—a world that they had come so close to. They were just seven miles away when their long journey ended in disaster. Just like Moses in the Bible, they had glimpsed the promise land but were not to enter it.

But even in this macabre scene of death and destruction, a few sparks of life still glowed. Mr. House, the ship's engineer, had stayed on board to help fight the fire, but when it became apparent that the ship was lost, he lowered himself over the side onto a door that floated nearby. Fearful that he might lapse into unconsciousness and drift away, he fastened his small island of refuge to the side of the ship by tying onto a timber dangling down the side of the ship. Mr. Donohue, the ship's purser, was at the stern of the ship hanging onto the rudder chains. Not far from House, a female passenger clung to a floating settee. Mr. House also noted a young man he recognized as a cabin boy sprawled out on a floating piece of debris; but he had not moved for a long time. House began to wonder if he was going to make it. The cold water was severely sapping his strength; it seemed like he had been in the water for hours. Hope was fading. He looked toward the floating debris where he had seen the boy; he was gone. He called out to the lady clinging to the settee trying to encourage her. She answered by feebly waving to him.

House struggled against the strong urge to close his eyes and float into delirium. Then he heard a sound; it was the steady splashing of oars dipping in and out of the water. He tried to clear his befuddled mind. Was it real or just a hallucination? Then suddenly it occurred to him: it's a boat; a rescue boat! From some deep untapped resource of energy, he was able to weakly call out and wave. The boats from shore had returned at last! But wait…it couldn't be the boats from shore; it was coming from the wrong direction for that. The young woman on the settee saw the boat as well; in her excitement, with rescue at hand, she lost her grip. She disappeared beneath the dark water without a sound. Within a few moments, the boat from the schooner *Liberty* pulled into view. House was not sure if it was real. The next thing he felt were the strong rough hands of sailors pulling him aboard the boat; the hands were real.

In just a few more moments, the steamer *Delaware* rushed into view. A boiling white bow wave indicated that it was speeding along under full steam. En route to the disaster scene, the crew ran excitedly about the rapidly moving steamer, gathering blankets and warm clothing and readying bunks for the expected flood of survivors. The cook aboard the *Delaware* soon had a large pot of hot coffee ready. As they drew closer to the *Phoenix*, the crew of the *Delaware* anxiously lined the rails as the steamer slowed. At the sight of the burnt-out derelict, the crew was shocked speechless. The full reality of the situation then struck them. There would be no rescue. The *Delaware* was passing through a watery graveyard. Many of the tough old sailors, with tears in their eyes, took off their hats and stood silently staring at the killing waters. Slowly, the *Delaware* circled the *Phoenix* in search of survivors, as did the boat from the *Liberty*. Then a sailor in the *Liberty*'s boat saw a movement under the stern of the burnt-out hulk. It was Donohue, the ship's clerk; the boat quickly moved in and pulled the half-frozen man from his refuge. On the *Delaware*, they spotted some floating timbers and heard a weak cry for help; there was a man in the water. With the utmost speed, a boat was lowered and the man was tenderly lifted into the boat. Later, the nearly frozen man was identified as a Mr. Long of Milwaukee. After an extensive search of the area, Captain Tuttle ordered them to stop looking. Three survivors were all that was left of the three hundred or more souls left to fend for themselves on the burning ship. About forty-five people had made it ashore in the two lifeboats. No reason was ever given for the boats not returning to the *Phoenix*. The Irish O'Conner family was one of the few families that survived the *Phoenix* disaster intact.

A stout towing cable was made fast to the *Phoenix*, and it was then taken under tow by the *Delaware*. The small steamer struggled to tow the dead weight of the blackened hulk. The fire had opened the seams of the *Phoenix*, and it was taking on water and getting heavier by the minute. After what seemed an eternity, the pier at Sheboygan hove into sight. The dawn of a new day was just breaking. Suddenly, the forepart of the structure on the *Phoenix* collapsed in a cloud of ash. The purser's safe was seen to tumble into the lake. As the *Delaware* slowly approached the Sheboygan pier, it looked as though the entire city had quietly lined the shore and crowded onto the pier.

The *Phoenix*, in a near sinking condition, was riding low, drawing much more water than the *Delaware*. The *Phoenix* was about to claim one more victim. Suddenly, the wreck grounded and stopped. Before the startled crew of the towing vessel could slack off the tow cable, it pulled tight and then parted with a bang like a cannon shot. The end of the cable attached to the *Delaware* whipsawed wickedly across the pier. People scattered; a few fell into the frigid lake. A seven-year-old boy standing on the pier stood stock still, rooted in fear. The slashing cable struck him savagely in the face, knocking him unconscious. At first it appeared he was dead; he was not. The badly injured lad was carried to a doctor's home for treatment. He recovered and lived to a ripe old age, but he forever bore the scars of that terrible night as the last victim of the *Phoenix*. The derelict ship then settled to the bottom. The *Phoenix* and the remains of some of the immigrants had at last arrived in Sheboygan.

The sun rose, announcing the arrival of a new day. The pristine waters of Lake Michigan sparkled under its golden rays. The cold pure waters of the lake gave no hint of the horror that had taken place on its surface fewer than twenty hours before. In Sheboygan, as soon as it was learned that the survivors of the *Phoenix* disaster were on the beach north of the city, a rescue party was organized. However, here the story of the *Phoenix* varies. Some accounts state that the survivors walked to Sheboygan; others say that wagons from Sheboygan found them huddled around a campfire. Whatever is the correct account, it is known that the survivors at last made it to Sheboygan and into the arms of family and friends.

Later that day, the schooner *Liberty* sailed to Milwaukee with news of the terrible tragedy. A recently installed telegraph line ran into the city, and when the news of the loss of the *Phoenix* was learned, it was flashed across the telegraph lines to every major city in the United States. Relief efforts and fundraising to help the survivors poured in. It took over three months for the news to reach Holland, and when it did a national day of morning was called. All across Holland, church bells pealed and memorial services were held.

The day after the loss of the *Phoenix*, the survivors of the crew were alarmed to hear dark mutterings that the disaster was due to a drunken crew. The crew men quickly booked passage on the *Delaware*, which was heading back to Buffalo. The next day, it sailed north. As the *Delaware* passed through the area where the *Phoenix* had burned, the lake was littered with floating bodies. Everyone expected Captain Tuttle to stop and recover the dead; he inexplicably made no such attempt and sailed on, much to the consternation of his crew and passengers. This decision was to haunt Captain Tuttle the rest of his days.

Captain Sweet, still suffering from his fall, was taken into the home of a local doctor, where he lived for almost a year. The doctor stated that Captain Sweet suffered severe melancholia. After he left the doctor's home, Captain Sweet returned to Buffalo, but he never commanded another ship.

As for the *Phoenix*, that winter it was covered with ice and torn in half, with the bow section ending up on the beach. The owners, Pease and Allen, had the engines removed once the ice melted the following spring and then

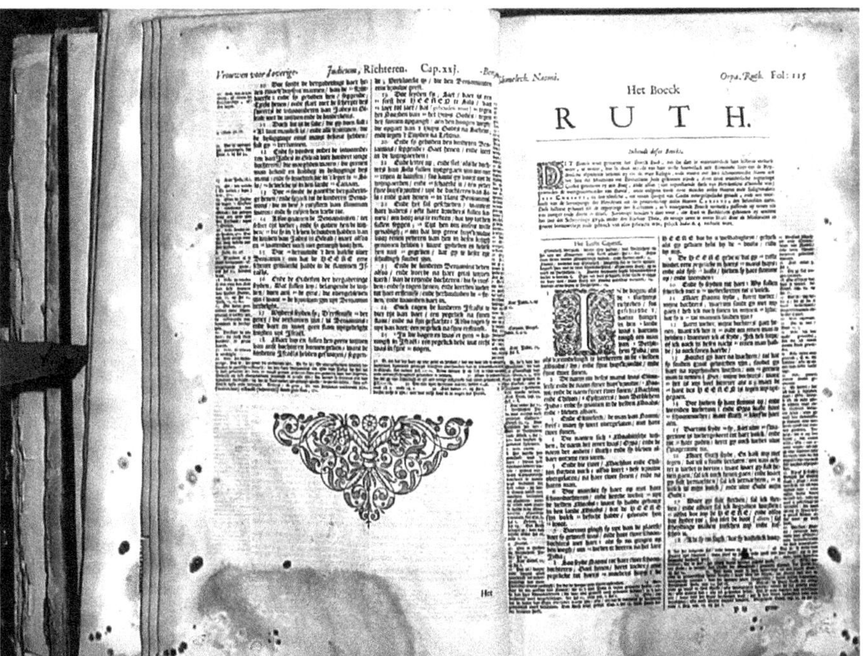

Richteren. Cap.xxj.

Het Boeck

R U T H.

All that remains of the *Phoenix* today is this water-stained Bible brought ashore by a survivor. *Courtesy Sheboygan County Historic Research Center.*

abandoned the hulk. As the lakefront changed and was filled in, the remains of the once proud ship were covered and today most likely lie beneath the parking lot across from the YMCA.

All that remains of the *Phoenix* is a large water-stained Bible that was carried ashore and is preserved at the Sheboygan Historical Research Center in Sheboygan Falls. Today, no ship on the Great Lakes carries the name *Phoenix*, as it is considered a voodoo name. Five ships had carried that name, and all sunk or were burned.

The *Phoenix* disaster is still a mystery to this day. Its cause will never be known for sure. Was it an overheated boiler? Or the inattention of a drunken crew, as suggested by some? Or was it just a simple clogging of the feed-water intake that supplied water to the boilers? The answers to these questions are lost to time.

Over the years, several attempts have been made to locate the site of the burning *Phoenix* in hopes of finding gold lost by the immigrants, but to no avail. Like the sites of so many other shipwrecks, Lake Michigan holds its secrets well.

A footnote to this story is that on November 12, 1855, the steamer *Delaware*, which came to the rescue of the *Phoenix*, was also lost near Sheboygan. It sprang a leak during a gale and went down with the loss of eleven persons.

DEATH IN AN ICY RIVER

The headline of the February 9, 1911 *Sheboygan Daily Press* cried in huge black type: "SHOCKING ACCIDENT."

On that frosty morning at about 8:40 a.m., well-known Sheboygan Captain William Groh was at the helm of his sturdy tug the *Peter Reiss*. The tug, which was now approaching the bridge that spanned the Sheboygan River at Eighth Street, gave several sharp blasts on its steam whistle, a signal to open the bridge. The Eighth Street Bridge in place at that time was a swing bridge; in other words, it was pivoted on its center, which was mounted on a heavy stone abutment in the center of the river. When opened, the whole bridge would swing so that it was parallel to the riverbank, allowing ships to pass on either side. There were usually two men on duty at the bridge. The bridge operator sat in a small control cab high atop the bridge, and an assistant, prior to the bridge opening, would string chains across the street to indicate that the bridge was open. The chains were not intended to physically stop vehicles from plunging through the open bridge but merely acted as a warning. On hearing the signal from the tug to open the bridge, the safety chains were put in place, and the bridge with a low growl began to grind slowly open.

The *Peter Reiss* and its crew on that late winter morning had been hired to break free a steamer that was still held in the grip of the frozen river. As the tug smashed its way through the ice toward the bridge, it came to a complete stop until the bridge was open. As the tug lay patiently waiting to pass the bridge, Captain Groh, in the wheelhouse atop the tug, cast a casual glance to his right up toward Eighth Street. The street at this location is a steady down grade for almost five blocks. As Captain Groh watched, he noticed a trolley car coming down the hill, at a speed he later estimated to be twenty miles per hour, directly toward the now completely open bridge. As Captain Groh continued to watch the trolley, he expected it to slow and then come to a complete stop—but it did not!

George Thieme, age thirty-seven, married with three children, had been a motorman with the Sheboygan Light and Power Company for just over six years. On this fateful day, he and a conductor, identified only as Mr. Weber, were assigned to the operation of car #54, which was headed south to the Lakeview Hotel that was located on a bluff overlooking Lake Michigan at the east end of Wilson Avenue.

At 8:45 a.m. on that cold morning of February 9, 1911, car #54 left the terminal of the trolley company, then located in the present-day 500 block of South Eighth Street. On board were seven persons: five passengers, the motorman Thieme and the conductor, Mr. Weber. As Thieme took over the car, he was informed that they were behind schedule and that he had only ten minutes to get to the end of the run, which was the Lake View Hotel. Furthermore, he had just an additional ten minutes to return to the terminal, a fact that would haunt the company during later inquiries. The passengers had no inkling of the horror that lay ahead, just moments away. Seated in the rear of the car were fifty-three-year-old Anna Mather, a schoolteacher from Sheboygan Falls, and twenty-year-old Tannie Van Ouwerkerk, a music teacher also from Sheboygan Falls. Toward the front of the trolley sat fourteen-year-old Olga Willimite, of Sheboygan. Just behind the motorman sat P.W. Etzold, a traveling salesman from Milwaukee. In the rear of the car, near where the two older ladies were seated, Joseph Mosich of Sheboygan had chosen a seat.

Car #54 turned left out of the terminal and headed south down the Eighth Street hill toward its fate. As the trolley approached the Eighth Street Bridge, motorman Thieme saw the chains drawn across the roadway ahead. Seeing the barrier, Thieme realized that the bridge was open and began to apply the brakes to the trolley car. To his horror, the brakes had no effect. In desperation, the motorman activated the sanders, which are devices that drop sand under the wheels of the trolley to give the wheels extra traction on the rails. Sanders were used only in extreme emergencies, because the abrasive action of the sand ground flat spots on the wheels, necessitating their costly replacement. For some reason, the sanders did not work, and the out-of-control trolley careened toward the yawning gap in the roadway caused by the open bridge. There was but one alternative left to the desperate motorman: throw the motors into reverse in an attempt to halt the car. Knowing that serious damage could be done by this action, he threw the motors into full reverse. But car #54 continued on toward the icy river.

At that point, Thieme yelled, "I can't hold her, everybody jump!" The two male passengers did not hesitate and jumped from the car, which now had begun to slow down. The three women sat frozen to their seats in terror. Again the motorman yelled, "Jump, jump," but the women did not move. Thieme felt the car begin to tip as it reached the end of the track. He said later that he had no idea how he left the car, but suddenly he found himself in the icy water clinging to a cake of ice. The conductor had also jumped and had landed in the river, but he was clinging desperately to pilings along the riverbank.

Witnesses later said that as the car hurtled into the opening, it turned slowly upside down before it struck the water. The trucks (wheels) separated from the trolley in midair. With a huge splash, car #54 sank into the river. As the trolley car settled, it righted itself, due to the weight of the motors and other running gear in the bottom of the car. Car #54 now lay on the bottom of the Sheboygan River in nine feet of water, with three passengers still on board and a small portion of its roof visible above water.

This unbelievable scenario took place directly in front of the stunned crew of the tug *Peter Reiss*. For just a moment, Captain Groh was frozen into inaction by the disaster taking place in front of him. But Captain Groh, a man of action, recovered his senses quickly. The first thing he saw was motorman Thieme floundering in the water.

The tug immediately moved forward and picked up the half-frozen motorman, who gasped as they pulled him aboard, "Three ladies are still in the car." Thieme, already suffering the effects of the bone-chilling water, was shivering uncontrollably. Having been informed that passengers were still aboard the trolley, Captain Groh quickly maneuvered the *Peter Reiss* alongside the nearly submerged car. Grabbing a fire axe, he sprang onto the

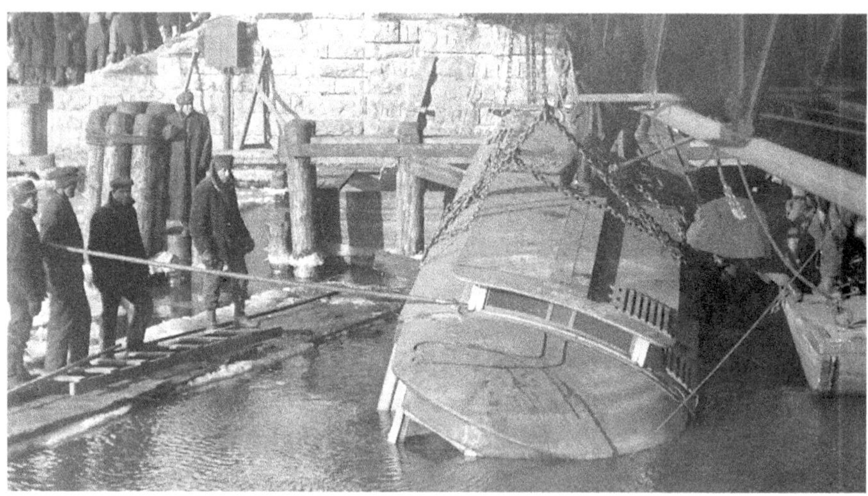

Slowly, car #54 is lifted from the river. *Courtesy Sheboygan County Historic Research Center.*

roof of car #54, closely followed by another crewman who also carried an axe. The two men began frantically chopping a hole in the roof of the trolley in hopes that someone inside might still be alive. As they were about to break through the roof, Captain Groh warned the other man to take caution, as there was a possibility they could injure passengers who might still be alive. As they gingerly broke through the roof, they found that the car was filled to the top with icy water, precluding the possibility of finding anyone inside alive. Captain Groh called for a boat hook from the tug. The boat hook is a long pole with a hook at its end and is frequently used to retrieve objects from the water.

With the boat hook, Groh began to probe inside the water-filled car. He soon snagged the inert body of Anna Mather and, with the aid of bystanders (by this time there were hundreds), pulled her from the wreck and passed her up to helping hands on the shore. Next, the body of Tannie Van Ouwerkerk was recovered, and last of all fourteen-year-old Olga Willimite was removed from car #54.

By any standard, motorman Thieme should have been considered a hero. The gallant operator stayed with the car and tried to stop the runaway vehicle with every resource at his command, until he nearly lost his own life in the ice-choked river.

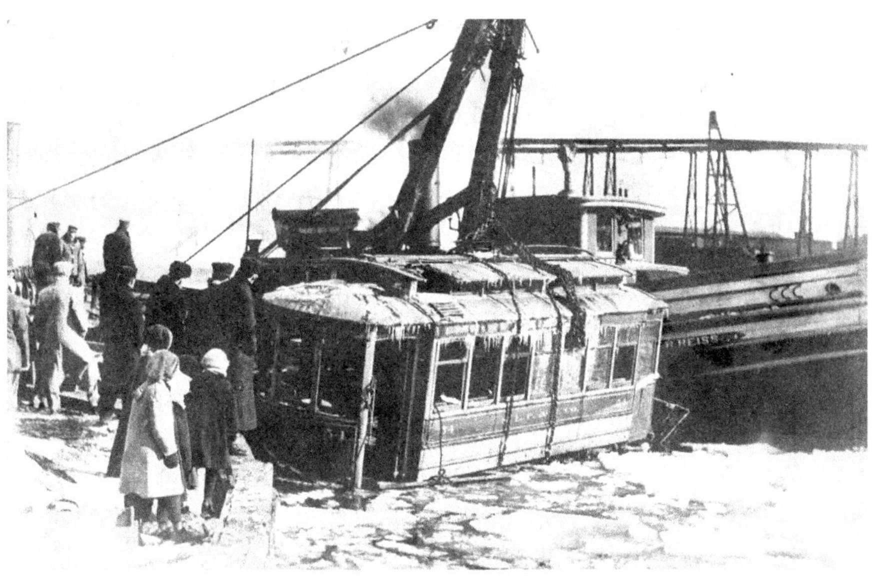

The tug *Peter Reiss* stands by while a crane lifts car #54 out of the Sheboygan River. *Courtesy Sheboygan County Historic Research Center.*

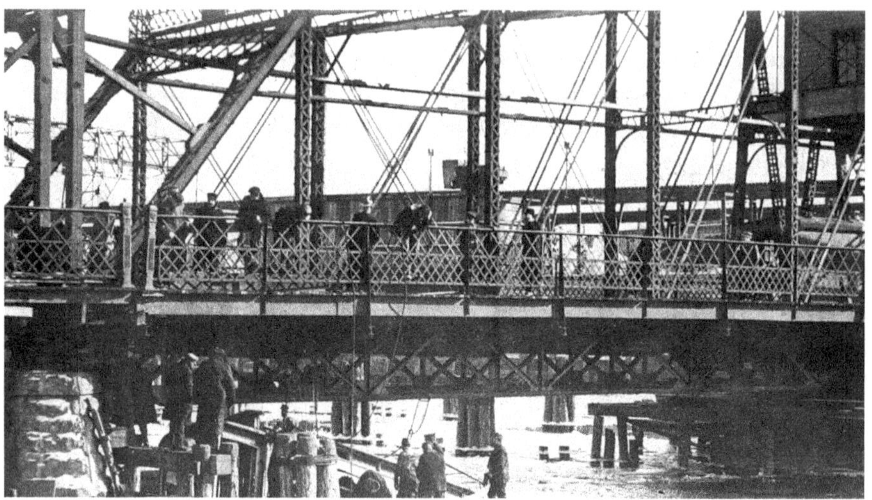

Curious crowds gather as rescue operations continue. *Courtesy Sheboygan County Historic Research Center.*

The recovery of the sunken trolley was still underway when ugly rumors began to circulate. It was rumored that Thieme was drunk; another said that he jumped out of the car two blocks from the drawbridge, and others said he was traveling downhill at a tremendous speed. All the rumors had one thing in common: they were false.

Investigators noted that on the morning of September 9, Sheboygan was covered with a heavy layer of frost, making even walking a hazard. With this information in mind, it is logical to assume that the trolley tracks were covered with frost, making it nearly impossible to stop. Furthermore, they also found several sections of track had sand spread on them, indicating that the sanders were working. As for the rumors of all the witnesses interviewed, not one could recall any action at the scene by Thieme that would indicate he was drunk. It was very clear that he had not jumped out two blocks away, as he was rescued from the river by Captain Groh. Captain Groh also said that when the car went into the river it had slowed to the speed "of a man walking." In testimony given later, Groh said, "If the car would have had ten more feet, it would have stopped."

On February 16, 1911, just nine days after the tragic trolley car accident, Sheboygan Police Chief August Sheck arrested motorman George Thieme on three counts of fourth-degree manslaughter. He then appeared in court and was bound over to circuit court, and bail was set at $800, which was paid for by the company.

On February 11, a coroner's inquest was called. The district attorney served over fifty subpoenas on witnesses who were to testify in the upcoming hearing. The hearing was convened on February 13, and dozens of witnesses testified, among them Captain Groh and George Thieme, who were grilled by the district attorney at great length. On February 15, the coroner's jury found Thieme guilty of three counts of fourth-degree manslaughter and sent the case on to circuit court.

The trial began in Sheboygan's old courthouse on April 15, with a standing-room-only crowd of spectators. Thieme again testified at great length, explaining to the jury every detail of his herculean effort to try and get the out-of-control trolley to stop; the jury listened with rapt attention. Captain Groh also described the heroic action of his tugboat crew during the disaster and their futile attempt to rescue the three ladies trapped in the sunken car. Dozens of other persons testified, including a Sheboygan alderman who happened to be working in the area at the time of the disaster. On April 18, the final witness testified and the case was given to the jury, who then left the courtroom to deliberate. At 9:00 a.m. the following day,

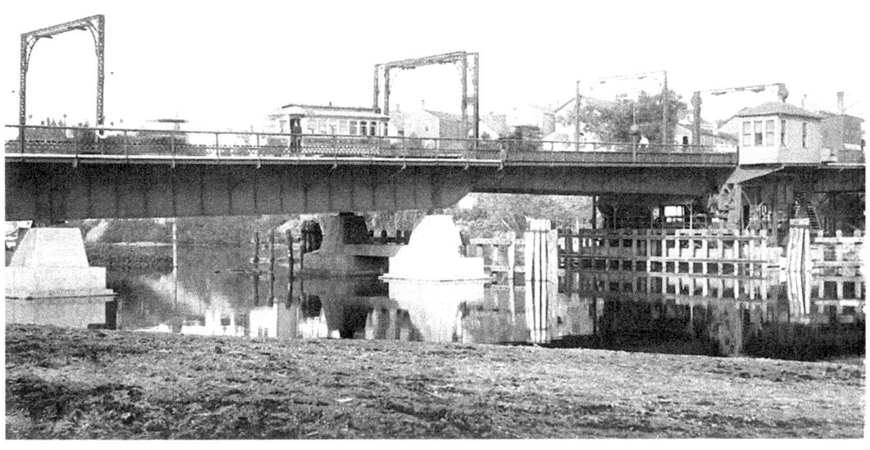

The trolley car shown is exactly the same type that carried three persons to their death in the icy river. *Author's collection.*

the jury notified the judge that they had reached a verdict, and the court was reconvened. The judge asked the foreman of the jury if they had reached a verdict; he answered, "Yes your honor we have." The judge then said, "The defendant will rise and face the jury." The judge ordered the foreman to read the verdict. In a strong voice, the foreman read, "We the jury find the defendant, George Thieme, not guilty as charged."

At last, the long nightmare was over for George Thieme.

The Pastor Is In

The Reverend William Wambsganss was the revered and respected pastor of the Bethlehem Lutheran Church that was, and still is, located at the corner of South Twelfth Street and Broadway Avenue in Sheboygan. The congregation was flourishing and the church was doing well. It seemed to the members of the church that Pastor Wambsganss was the perfect man to lead their flock.

The pastor and his family lived nearby in a large, comfortable home provided by the church. On the second floor, he had a large study where he prepared his sermons and met with church members who called at his home. All in all, the pastor was leading a comfortable and satisfying existence. Life was good for the pastor on that sunny spring day of June 9, 1927.

The life of Frank Doering Sr. and family, who lived a short distance from Reverend Wambsganss, could not have been more different in every way. In direct contrast to the pastor's family, the Doering family was deeply troubled. They had lost their oldest son in World War I, a loss they were deeply affected by. Their younger son Walter, for reasons not explained, had very difficult relations with his father. Neither of the two families in their most terrifying nightmares could have foreseen the horrendous circumstances that were about to engulf them on that pleasant June day.

Later, Mrs. Doering would recall that Walter seemed very quiet and withdrawn that day. She recalled that about 11:00 a.m. she had sent him on an errand to the grocery store and that when he returned home he dropped the bags on the kitchen table and turned and left the house without saying a word to her. Mrs. Doering also recalled that earlier in the day she heard her husband chopping wood in the basement. After a while the chopping stopped, but her husband did not come upstairs. At first she made nothing of this, thinking that perhaps he was working on some other project. At about 11:45 a.m., she became somewhat concerned and called down the

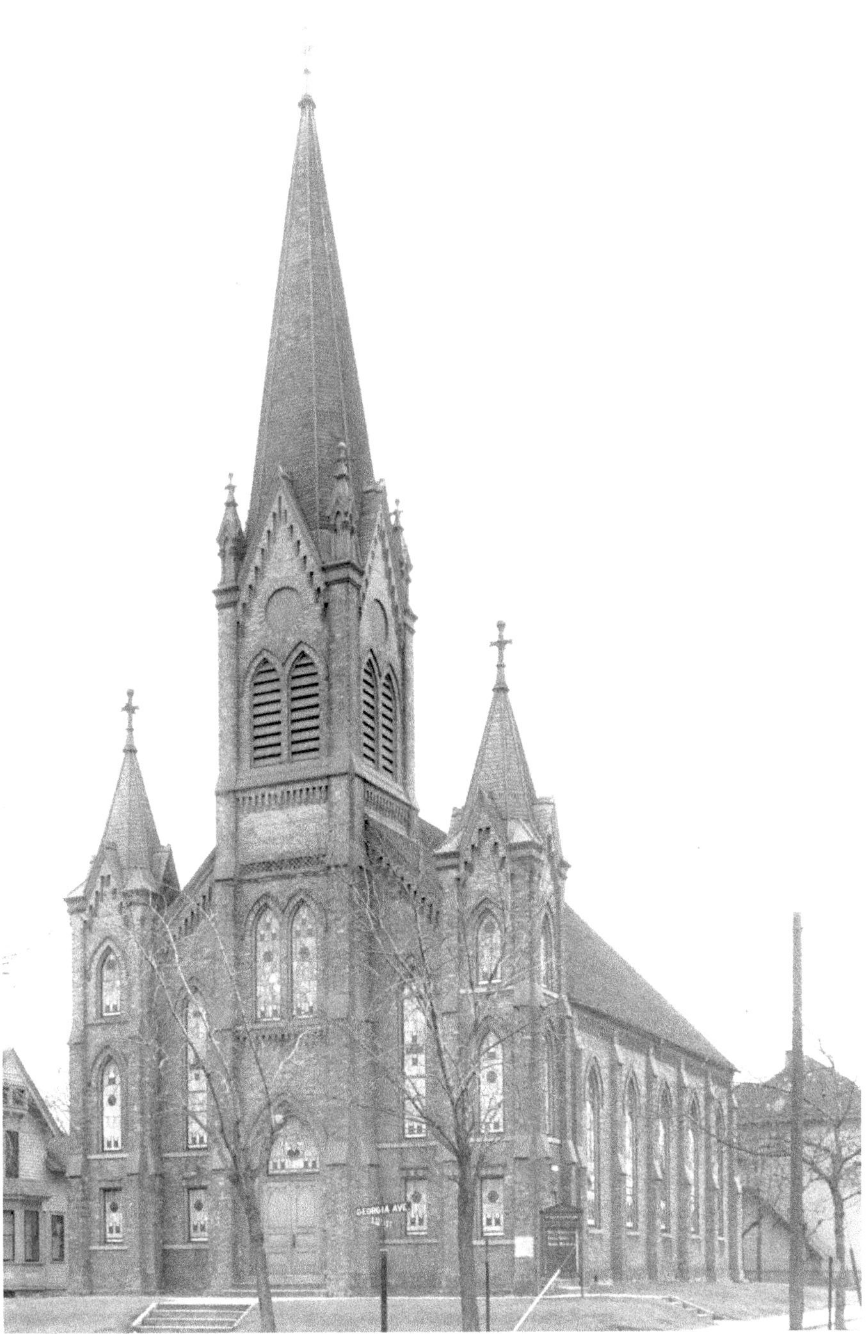

Bethlehem Lutheran Church. *Courtesy Sheboygan County Historic Research Center.*

steps to her husband, Frank. Hearing no response from him, she went down to the basement to investigate and to retrieve some items that she needed. As she walked down the basement steps, she suddenly stopped dead in her tracks and was horrified to find the body of her husband sprawled on the basement floor in a large pool of blood. The terrified woman ran back up the steps and called her family physician, Dr. Emil Gunther, who lived just a short distance away. Within a few minutes, Dr. Gunther arrived and rushed into the basement. After a quick examination of the body of Frank Doering, the doctor declared that he was deceased. The cause of death was a gunshot wound to the head. No weapon was present, which tended to indicate that it was not a self-inflicted wound. Dr Gunther called the police and the coroner. When the police arrived, due to the circumstances, they treated the scene as a homicide. As the police began their investigation, all members of the Doering family were present. All, that is, except young Walter, and his whereabouts were unknown.

On that same morning at about 11:00 a.m., the Wambsgansses received a phone call from a young man, later believed to be Walter Doering, inquiring if the pastor was in. When he was informed that the pastor was, the young man hung up. A short time later, Walter Doering appeared at the Wambsganss home asking to see the pastor, but the reverend had just stepped out for a moment, and the young man was informed that he would return in about thirty minutes. At about 11:45 a.m., Walter Doering again appeared at the parsonage. This time, Pastor Wambsganss was in, and Walter was shown upstairs to his study. The pastor greeted Walter at the top of the stairs, and the two men disappeared behind closed doors. At about noon, the pastor's family had lunch without him, as his guest still had not left. At about 12:30 p.m., the reverend's son, needing some papers from his father's office, went upstairs, stopped outside the closed door and listened. Hearing no voices, the puzzled young man knocked and then opened the door. As he stepped into the room, the pastor's son was confronted by a horrifying scene. On the floor in a large pool of blood lay the contorted body of young Walter Doering, with a gunshot wound to his head. At his desk, the Reverend Wambsganss was also found dead of a gunshot wound to the head. A blood-spattered Bible lay open on the pastor's desk, from which it seems he may have been reading. On the floor near the body of Walter Doering lay a .32-caliber revolver that had been fired three times.

No inquest was ever held by authorities into the tragic deaths of the three men. Many questions still remain unanswered: did Walter kill his father and then go to the home of the pastor and, for some unknown reason, kill him and then himself? Or did Mr. Doering kill himself and then Walter discovered the body, picked up the weapon and went to the pastor's home to arrange for his father's burial? Many times, in those days, the Lutheran Church would refuse to bury people who had died by their own hand. Is this what happened when Walter requested burial? And did he then, in a fit of rage, kill the pastor and then himself? What happened behind those closed doors will never be known.

CHAPTER 2

TALES OF MURDER

THE LAST PATROL

Police work, though risky, is not inherently dangerous, as most of us have been led to believe. Men who work off the back of a garbage truck and cab drivers who work at night have a far higher fatality rate than the average police officer. One of the most dangerous occupations is to work in a mini-mart after midnight.

During his entire career, the average officer never fires his side arm in anger and makes only one serious felony arrest. Most of what a police officer does on a routine day is just that—routine. It is this very boring routine that can be deadly, for it can engender an attitude that "nothing can happen to me." In my twenty-eight-year career as a police officer, I was very fortunate to have never fired my gun in anger and drew it only a very few times. Officer Theodore Husting of the Sheboygan Police Department was not as fortunate as I.

In years past, walking the beat is what a police officer did. He patrolled his assigned district on foot, a task I performed many times. Often, on a cold rainy night at 3:00 a.m., it caused a person to wonder what in the world you were doing out there. Your main task was to "rattle doorknobs," check for possible burglaries and to interrogate and keep records of any suspicious person found wandering about in an area where he didn't belong.

On the fiftieth anniversary of the death of Officer Husting, I had a chance to meet and talk with his wife at a memorial service given by the Sheboygan Police Department in his honor. Mrs. Husting related that her husband Ted

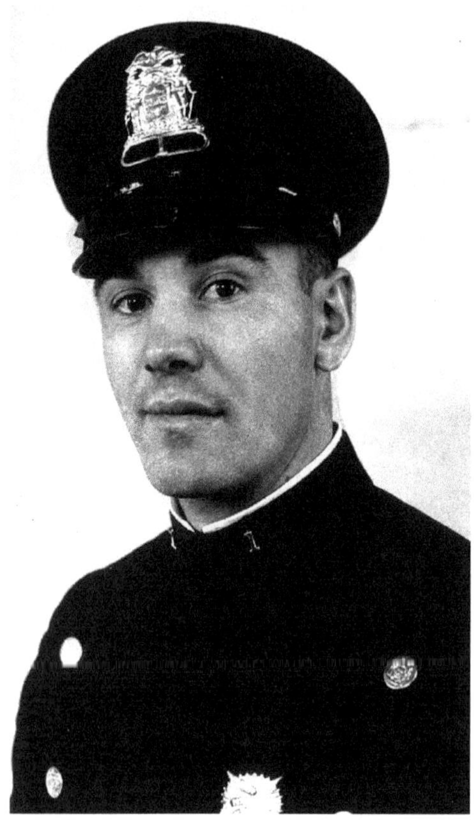

Officer Theodore Husting. *Courtesy Sheboygan County Historic Research Center.*

told her that since he was a small boy he wanted to be a cop. She said Ted told her that he used to sit in the front yard and wait for the officer on the beat to pass his home, and then he would walk along with him as far as he could. Mrs. Husting said that she clearly remembered the day her husband received word that the application he had submitted to the Sheboygan Police Department for the position of police officer had been accepted, and how excited he was. She further reminisced about how proud he felt the first time he donned his new uniform and the apprehension and excitement he experienced as Sheboygan's newest police officer.

On October 23, 1930, Ted Husting proudly joined the ranks of the Sheboygan Police Department as a "special" officer. At that time, when a young man was accepted by the department, he was classified as a special officer. This meant that he more or less worked in a part-time capacity, such as filling in for someone who might be sick, working at a special event such as the Fourth of July or maybe being called out to assist at a large fire for crowd control. Then when someone retired or left the department, the special officer would move up on the list of specials until he reached the top of the list. When the next opening occurred for a regular officer, he would be sworn in as a regular and would become a full-time police officer. On February 2, 1931, Theodore Husting became a fully sworn full-time Sheboygan police officer. Again according to Viola Husting, her twenty-seven-year-old husband had at last realized his boyhood dream—he was a cop. It was tradition on the Sheboygan PD that the newest officers were assigned to the midnight to 8:00 a.m. shift. As an officer increased his seniority, he would advance to the 4:00 p.m. to midnight shift, and then after about ten years he at last would advance to the day shift, which worked from 8:00 a.m. to 4:00 p.m. During his entire six-and-a-half-year career, Ted worked nights.

The winter of 1937 was a cold one. Temperatures constantly dipped into the single digits and at times below zero. Saturday night, March 27, 1937, was no exception. The weather report called for partly cloudy weather and cold. As usual, Ted arrived at the police station about thirty minutes before the start of his shift. Under his long, heavy police coat, he would have worn a sweater and certainly the warmest long underwear he could find and maybe even two pairs of socks. Roll call took place at 11:45 p.m., during which the officers were briefed on any problems they were to look out for and given a list of stolen cars that might be in the area or wanted persons to watch out for. On that night, Officer Husting was assigned to beats three, four and five, which were located on the northeast side of Sheboygan. It was not uncommon for officers to be assigned to several beats when much of the area they were to patrol was residential, as was the case with Husting's beat that fateful night.

Walking the beat on a cold winter's night is a lonely and unrewarding job. The officer must endlessly make the rounds, checking doors and being alert to suspicious persons or circumstances. In short, it is boring and tedious, as much of police work is, punctuated by a few moments of terror now and then. As Ted left the station, he probably walked north on North Ninth Street to Michigan Avenue, west to North Thirteenth Street and then north to Calumet Drive and Lincoln Avenue, checking doors all the way. At Calumet Drive and Lincoln Avenue, he would have made his first hourly "pull." The term "pull" meant that each hour the officer assigned to a specific area would go to one of the police call boxes that were located throughout the city. The call boxes were large gray boxes mounted on a short metal pole and almost always located on a corner. After the patrolman unlocked the box, he would pull down a lever inside the box and, by doing so, send a signal to police headquarters, which then punched out a paper tape indicating that he was on the beat and safe. The tape also indicated the patrolman's location. This task had to be performed every hour. Also in the box was a small telephone that the officer could use to summon help or contact the shift commander, if needed. Basically, an officer was pretty much on his own. If he discovered a crime in progress, he could either try to handle it alone or run to the nearest call box to summon help. If he chose the second option, the guilty party might escape; if he chose to apprehend the culprit himself, he could be putting himself in jeopardy, especially if the suspect were armed. It was a difficult decision to make, but it was one that the beat patrolman had to make many times.

At about 3:00 a.m., Patrolman Husting found himself at North Twelfth and Lincoln Avenue, where several business places were located. On the southwest corner was Moeller's Grocery. As he had done dozens of times earlier that night, he stepped up to the door, tried the doorknob and found it securely locked. He then shone his flashlight into the interior; everything inside appeared to be in order. The officer then moved to the shop next door, DeKarskes Shoe Repair, and the next, Connie's Battery and Electric Shop. All was in order. He then walked east across North Twelfth Street and checked the Nerlich Printing Co. and Stiller Cigar Co., and again, all was secure. Officer Husting now approached the southeast corner of North Twelfth and Lincoln, where Herman and Nehrings Tavern was located at 1135 Lincoln Avenue. Patrolman Husting could not have known this was to be no routine door check.

As usual, he walked up to the door, checked to see if it was locked and then shone his flashlight into the dark interior of the tavern. The small beam of his flashlight swept across the bar and then toward the west wall of the barroom, where several pinball machines stood in a row. It was at that moment that the officer saw the dark outline of a man run toward the rear of the tavern.

As the officer approached the building, twenty-eight-year-old Norbert Jocis was inside trying to pry open the coin box of a pinball machine. It was later learned that Jocis had been a customer of the bar earlier that evening. Jocis had in fact spent over four hour's playing cards and drinking until the bar closed at 1:00 a.m. It was later learned from Jocis himself that while he was in the bar, he slipped unseen into a back room and unlocked one of the windows with the intention of coming back later to burglarize the tavern after it closed. Jocis later stated that he came back to the tavern at about 2:30 a.m. and crawled in through the window he had unlocked. Once in the tavern, he immediately went to the cash register, opened the drawer and found only a small amount of coins; the proprietor had apparently removed the paper money upon closing. The young thief then began to rummage around behind the bar and found a loaded Colt .45-caliber military-type automatic pistol and a blackjack. He put the blackjack in his pocket, carried the gun out from behind the bar, laid it on a table and went to work on the pinball machine with a screwdriver. As he pried on the machine, Jocis was suddenly startled to see the beam of a flashlight sweep across the bar. Jocis dropped the screwdriver, picked up the gun and ran for the back of the bar with the intention of escaping out the window that he had originally entered. At this point, he was not aware that the officer had seen him.

But Officer Husting had seen the young burglar as he fled toward the rear of the tavern. The officer drew his gun, ran to the back of the tavern and peered into a window, where he again saw the shape of a man ducking into a side room. Officer Husting ran to a window located in the side room and shouted at the dark figure he saw inside, "Come out or I'll shoot." At this point, the story becomes somewhat confused, as Jocis later claimed that the officer fired three shots at him first and that he panicked and returned fire, and in the ensuing exchange of gunshots Officer Husting was fatally wounded. Jocis claimed he had no idea the officer was hit and his only thought was to escape, so he climbed out of the window he had used to enter the tavern.

Having been severely wounded in the abdomen, Officer Husting staggered out into the middle of North Twelfth Street and collapsed. Neighbors, awakened by the sound of gunfire, looked out of their windows and saw what appeared to be a man lying in the middle of the street. Not only was there someone lying in the street, but residents heard him cry out, "Help, help, I'm dying." Several of the neighbors rushed outside and were shocked to see that the prone figure of a man was in fact a police officer. As shaken onlookers knelt beside the wounded officer, he said, "Somebody shot me from George's & George's tavern, call my wife…2558-W…and call the police department…30." A female bystander ran back into her house and called Mrs. Husting. It was in this manner that she learned that her husband had been shot. This lady then called the police department, but several other persons had already called and she was informed that an ambulance and police were on the way. One of the first officers to arrive on the scene was Sergeant Ambrose Kiernan, who later said that when he arrived Officer Husting was still holding his gun in his hand and that it was cocked. In those days, the ambulance was run by the police department. When the ambulance

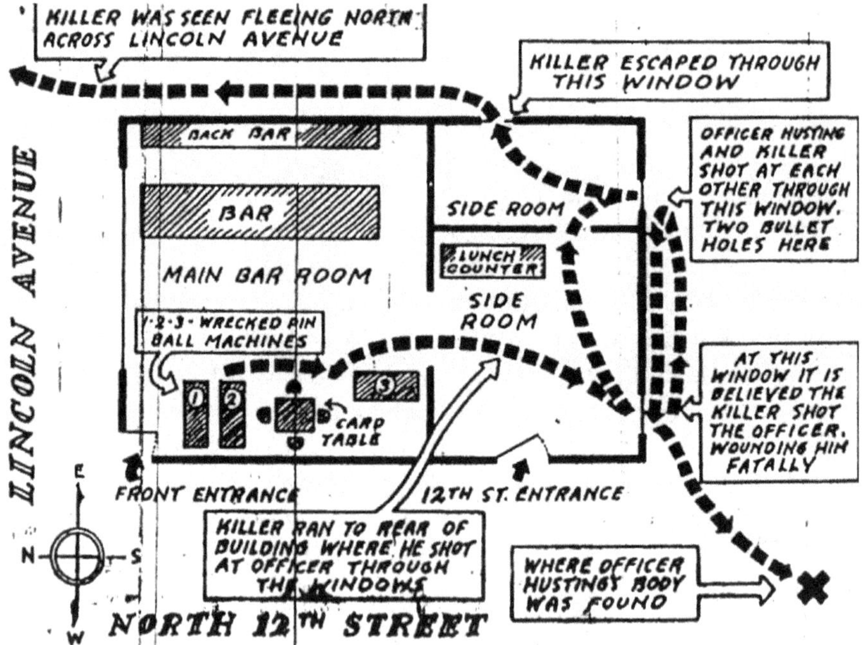

This diagram, which appeared in the local media, depicts the crime scene where Officer Husting was killed. *Author's collection.*

attendants bent down to lift their wounded comrade onto the cot, he looked up at his fellow policemen and said, "Gee Ham it hurts. Will you open my belt?" Officer Husting was then rushed to St. Nicholas Hospital, where he died at 4:23 a.m. The fatal shot had caused severe internal bleeding, and even though he was rushed into surgery upon arrival at the hospital, the bleeding could not be stopped.

Chief of Police Walter Wagner had been summoned, and he immediately ordered that all detectives be called out and rushed to the scene. Investigators found the open window in the side room and footprints in the thin layer of snow leading away from the crime scene. Detectives had no trouble at all following the tracks through backyards to the home of Norbert Jocis, who lived at 1127 Bluff Avenue, which was only a few blocks from the tavern. While they were following the tracks to the Jocis home, they found a piece of cloth that appeared to have been torn from someone's trousers as he climbed over a fence. Also at this location, they found a small handful of coins amounting to one dollar. Detectives assumed that the coins had been dropped by the burglar and were part of the loot; in fact, they were the entire loot!

When detectives arrived at the home where the tracks in the snow had led them, they began pounding on the door. After a short time, Mrs. Jocis answered the door. Detectives demanded to see her husband. She said that he was in bed sleeping. Officers then entered the home, and Norbert Jocis walked into the kitchen. Detectives noted that for a man who was supposed to have been sleeping he seemed very much wide awake. When Jocis said that he had been in bed since 1:30 a.m., his wife nodded in agreement. Permission was granted to search the home; however, after a search of several hours, nothing was found. Detective William Rothe standing in the kitchen of the Jocis home noted that they had an old-fashioned combination gas and wood stove. Looking at the stove, Rothe's eye was caught by the stove's large ashbin. Sliding the ashbin out, the detective immediately noted how heavy it was. Stirring through the cold ashes the sharp-eyed investigator discovered a Colt .45 automatic pistol and a blackjack, both of which were reported stolen from behind the bar at the tavern. The gun was later proven to be the murder weapon.

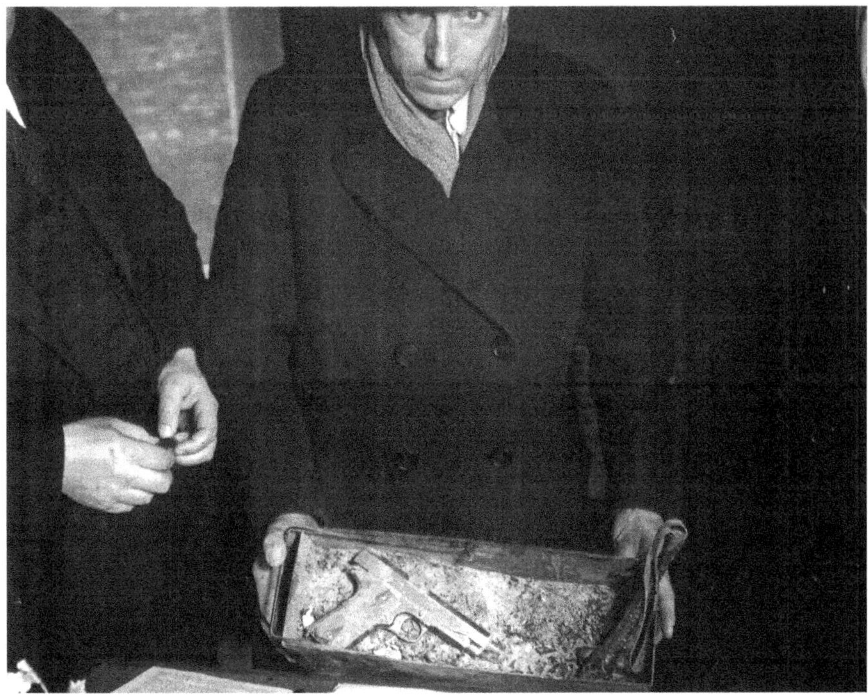

Detective William Rothe displays the murder weapon and blackjack he found in Jocis's ashbin. *Author's collection.*

Officers immediately took Jocis into custody and performed a paraffin test on his hands, which proved that he had recently fired a gun. After a lengthy interrogation by Chief Wagner and the district attorney, Jocis broke down and gave a complete confession.

Norbert Jocis was charged with second-degree murder, and a trial was set to begin on May 24, 1937. A jury was impaneled, and the next day the trial began. Just three days later, on May 26, all the witnesses had been heard and the jury began to deliberate. After five hours the jury contacted the judge and informed him they had reached a verdict. The defendant, Jocis, his attorney and the district attorney filed back into a near-empty courtroom. One of the only spectators present was the wife of Jocis. Judge Detling then asked the foreman of the jury if they had reached a verdict. He replied, "Yes, your honor, we have." The judge then said, "The defendant will rise and face the jury." The judge then said, "Please read your findings," to which the foreman of the jury replied, "We the jury, find Norbert Jocis guilty of murder in the second degree." The wife of Norbert Jocis buried her head in her hands and cried out, "No!" Judge Detling then set a date for sentencing. It was later learned that after they finished their deliberations, the members of the jury had cast only one ballot to arrive at their verdict. On May 28, 1937, Norbert Jocis, then twenty-eight, was sentenced by Judge Detling to a term of fourteen to twenty years and was immediately transported by the sheriff to the Wisconsin State Prison at Waupon.

On March 30, 1937, a funeral was held for Officer Theodore Husting. Officers from throughout the Midwest attended, along with hundreds of his Masonic brothers who, after the religious rites were completed, conducted a full Masonic burial rite. Along the entire route to the cemetery, hundreds of silent spectators lined the streets. It was later said that this was probably the largest funeral the city had ever seen.

One of the bitter ironies of the young officer's death was the fact that Officer Husting died for less than one dollar in coins, which his murderer lost in his desperate attempt to escape.

A Shooting at the Casino

One of the strangest sentences in the history of Sheboygan County for the crime of shooting another person was handed down on the shooting and eventual death of a young man named Arman McWilliams.

By June 1929, the full implications of the Volstead Act, better known as Prohibition, were beginning to become clear to the 100-plus taverns in the city. In the year 1929, it seems that Sheboygan had acquired a rather tarnished reputation based on two facts: the number of taverns in the city and the number of houses of ill repute, all of which operated openly in the city and county with little or no hindrance from authorities. It's interesting to note that in the year 1918, the year before Prohibition, over 120 taverns operated in the city. In 1920, the year that Prohibition became effective, the city directory showed 120 "soft drink parlors." Its curious how the city tavern owners, who continued to operate openly, had almost overnight convinced all their patrons to shun "demon rum" and drink only soft drinks. It was in this time frame that the following tale took place.

On the quiet Sunday morning of June 23, 1929, the Sheboygan County sheriff received a call at 5:45 a.m. that a shooting had taken place and a man was down at a roadhouse named the Casino. The Casino was famous, or infamous according to your point of view, as a speakeasy and house of ill repute and was located on the west side of what is now the 3600 block of Business Drive. There is now a large gas station and mini-mart at this location.

The call had been placed by the owner of the Casino, Kelly Howell, who was described by the media as a gambler and tavern operator. Sheriff

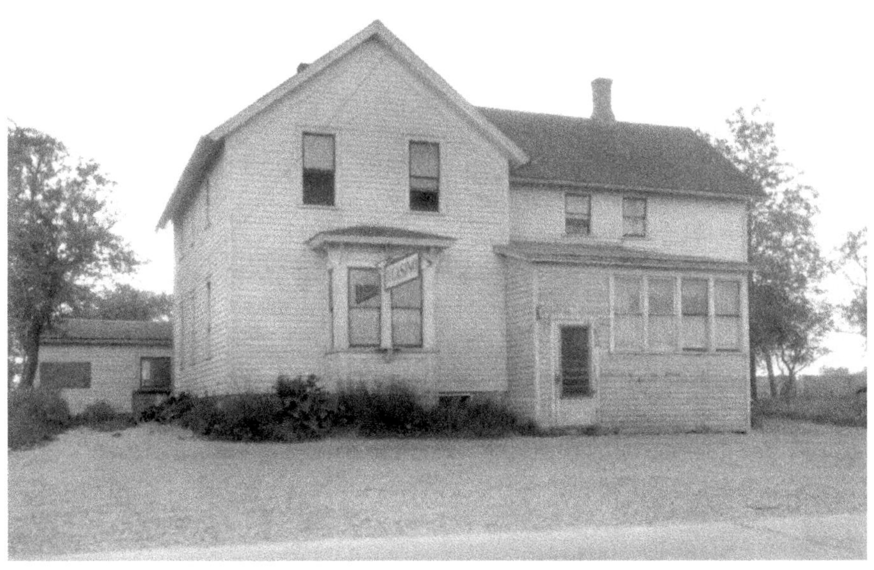

The Casino Roadhouse, the scene of the murder of Arman MacWilliams. *Courtesy Sheboygan County Historic Research Center.*

Louis Tasche responded to the call. Arriving at the Casino, he entered the establishment through a door that led to a front porch. Just inside the door, the sheriff found a young man lying on the porch floor with what appeared to be a gunshot wound to the abdomen. The victim was unconscious but appeared to be alive. The sheriff then entered the bar itself and summoned an ambulance to transport the seriously wounded young man to St. Nicholas Hospital. The victim was identified as twenty-three-year-old Arman McWilliams of Sheboygan.

As soon as the ambulance had been called, the proprietor of the Casino rushed up to the sheriff and told him he had shot McWilliams in self-defense. The sheriff noted that there were several other persons in the bar, all of whom had been witnesses to the shooting. The sheriff, quite naturally, assumed that with the tavern owner's blurted-out confession and the number of witnesses present this would be an open and shut case. He couldn't have been more wrong!

The sheriff warned the witnesses not to leave the premises until he could get a statement from each of them. Kelly Howell was the first to be interviewed. Howell related that he was working behind the bar of his tavern when at about 5:30 a.m. Arman McWilliams and several friends came into the bar. Howell said that as soon as he saw them, he realized that McWilliams and his buddies were drunk, which, according to Howell, meant big trouble. Howell said later that McWilliams had a reputation of being a mean drunk and that he feared for his safety. Howell related that he and McWilliams had, as he put it, "bad blood" between them. It seems that several months before, Howell had accused McWilliams of stealing three jugs of moonshine from his basement, an accusation that McWilliams denied.

On the day of the shooting, not wanting any trouble with McWilliams, Howell ordered him and his friends out of the bar, but McWilliams refused. Howell then related that McWilliams started toward him in a threatening manner and began to come around the end of the bar. It might be noted that McWilliams was a good deal younger than Howell and larger in stature, giving Howell good reason to fear him. Howell then picked up a .25-caliber automatic he kept behind the bar for just such occasions. Some witnesses claimed later that at this point Howell said, "Stop or I'll shoot," to which McWilliams is said to have replied, "Go ahead shoot me." Howell then fired one shot, hitting McWilliams in the abdomen. Some of the witnesses said that the wounded man staggered back and leaned against the wall for a few seconds and then walked to a table, sat down and put his head down on his arms and seemed to pass out. After a short time, McWilliams got up, went out on the porch, sat down and passed out on the floor, where, after having been called, the sheriff found him.

Sheriff Tasche then interviewed the other witnesses, one by one. The more stories he heard from witnesses the more confused he became. One bar patron said that McWilliams was "sober as a judge" when he came in, another said he was "drunk as a skunk" and yet another said he heard no gunshot and didn't know there was a shooting until the sheriff arrived. One of the bar patrons said McWilliams made no threatening moves toward Howell whatsoever and that he shot him with no warning, adding that, in his opinion, Howell shot McWilliams over the three jugs of missing moonshine. After the sheriff collected all the stories from the bar patrons, Kelly Howell was taken into custody on a charge of "assault with intent to do great bodily harm" and transported to the county jail. The following day, Howell made an appearance in court, was arraigned and bail was set at $3,000, which Howell posted; he was then released pending a hearing.

But Sheriff Tasche had a real dilemma: he had a gunshot victim, a confessed shooter and witnesses galore, none of whom could agree. But what he didn't have was a clear understanding of what had taken place in the shabby roadhouse or, for that matter, a motive.

When the ambulance arrived at St. Nicholas Hospital with the wounded McWilliams, the doctor on call realized that he was in very serious condition and would need immediate surgery, and he called for a surgeon. Dr. Conrad Tasche, a well-known Sheboygan surgeon, arrived a short time later. After a quick examination, Dr. Tasche stated that the patient was in grave danger and ordered him into surgery. After emergency surgery, McWilliams's condition just did not seem to improve, and it was feared that he might soon die. With this in mind, the district attorney felt compelled to take a dying declaration from McWilliams so as to get his version of what had taken place that fateful day. The statement later on was questioned, as Howell's attorney claimed that McWilliams had not been advised that his death was imminent. However, on June 28, just five days after he was shot, Arman McWilliams seemed to be improving. Dr. Tasche advanced the opinion that he was reasonably sure that McWilliams was going to survive. Early in the morning of July 1, 1929, twenty-three-year-old Arman McWilliams died. What had been a case of assault with intent to do great bodily harm was now a case of murder.

Kelly Howell was rearrested and charged with murder in the first degree. He was again held in the county jail until a hearing could be held. Bail was set at $10,000. On July 5, a coroner's jury was impaneled, and the facts surrounding the alleged murder were presented to them. After listening to all the facts and reading McWilliams's questionable dying declaration, the jury declared that the shooting of Arman McWilliams, which caused his death, was unjustified and that therefore a crime had taken place. Kelly Howell was bound over to circuit court and held in the county jail, with no bail being set. McWilliams's attorney appealed this decision in a plea to the circuit court. After considering the plea, the judge kept the bail at $10,000.

The trial of Kelly Howell on the charge of first-degree murder began in mid-September 1929. From the very onset of the trial, the case presented by the state was in trouble. Witness after witness was called by the state, many of them contradicting one another. Some, on recall to the stand, contradicted their own testimony. And then there was the contested dying declaration of McWilliams, which Howell's attorney claimed was invalid. After two weeks of testimony, the case at last went to the jury for deliberation on September 24. Prior to the jury retiring, the presiding judge's charge to the jury took thirty-five minutes to read. The judge explained to the jurors that they had six different charges to consider, and in his opinion first-degree murder was not one of them because the state had failed to prove its case. After a long deliberation, the jurors informed the judge that they were deadlocked at nine to three for conviction. The judge refused to accept their report and sent them back to deliberate once more. Again, after twenty hours the jurors reported they were hopelessly deadlocked at seven to five for conviction. At this point, the judge dismissed the jury.

The district attorney assured everyone that Howell would be retried. After months of wrangling, the charges against Howell were reduced to fourth-degree murder, to which Howell agreed to plead guilty. On May 7, 1930, Kelly Howell pled guilty in court to fourth-degree manslaughter, was assessed a $750 fine, which he paid, and walked out of court a free man.

THE DEATH OF A NATURALIST

As you drive down the scenic road leading into Sheboygan County Marsh, just before you enter the park area look to your left and you may see a small marker indicating that this is the site of the cabin owned by John Sexton. And just who was John Sexton? Much like the famous John Muir in California, John L. Sexton was a naturalist. As an old man, John could often be seen wandering the fields and forests near the marsh, collecting specimens of the flora and fauna of Sheboygan County. I am sure if John L. Sexton would

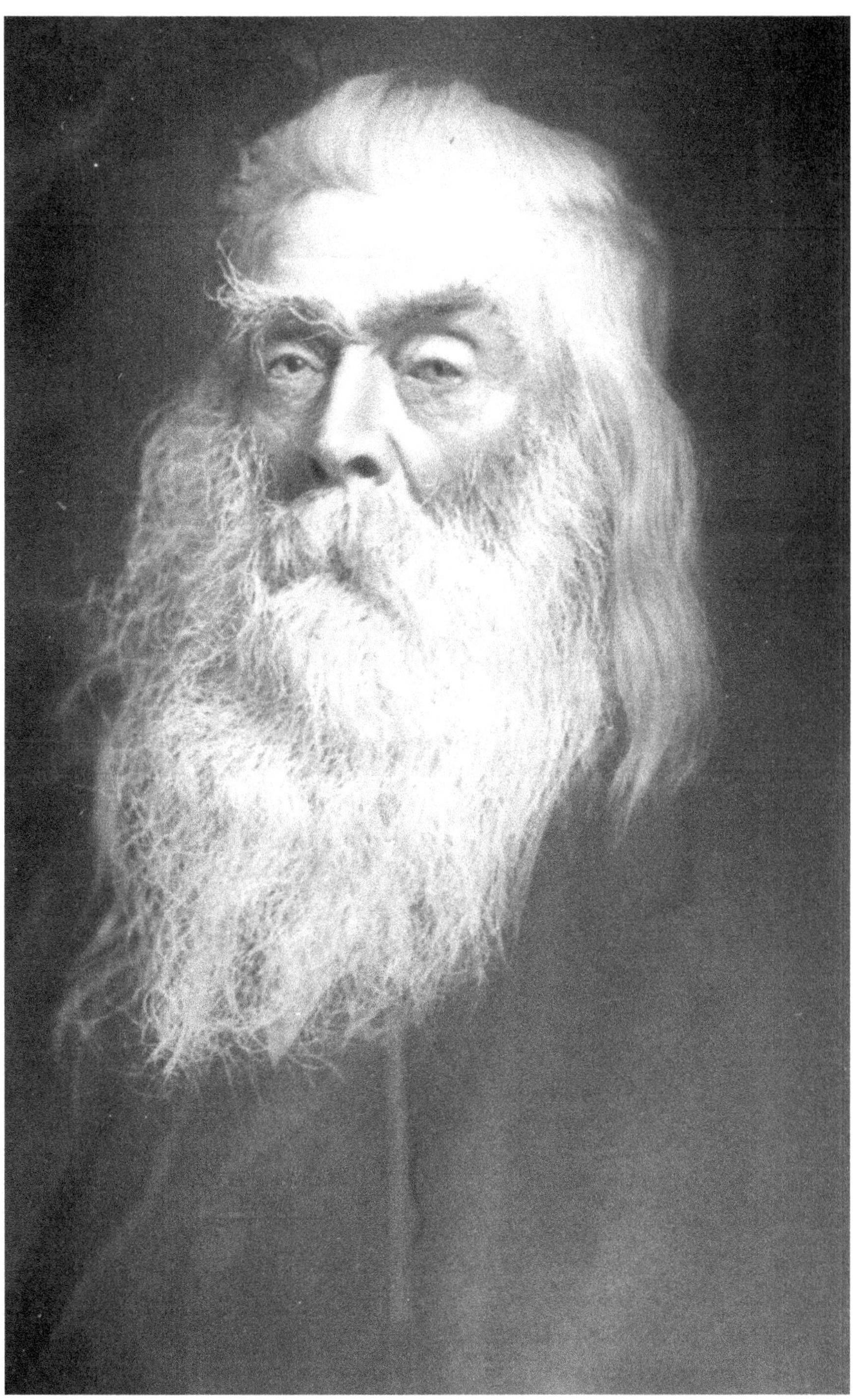

Murder victim John Sexton. *Courtesy Sheboygan County Historic Research Center.*

have been given a choice as to how he would like to be remembered, it would be as a teacher, scholar and friend of the outdoors.

Born in 1822, John came to the township of Russell in 1851, where he became the first postmaster and schoolteacher in the township. The young man began teaching school in a crudely built one-room log schoolhouse in section 12 of the town of Russell, on a road that today is named after him. It was not uncommon for him to have upward of thirty students at a time and be teaching eight different grades at once.

John married and had three sons and one daughter. Besides being postmaster, the young family man later became a justice of the peace in the town of Russell. As can be seen from a report John sent to the government, the job of postmaster was not a time-consuming one. A report submitted by him for the period of September 30 to December 31, 1862, showed that $1.93 was collected for postage. His commission was $1.52, and the balance due the government came to $0.41. During the succeeding quarter, he did a bit better: he collected $3.21 in postage, his commission was $2.46 and he submitted $0.75 to the government.

When not teaching or working in the post office, John was a familiar sight around the marsh and Elkhart Lake, notebook in hand recording his observations as he wandered through his beloved Kettle Moraine hills. John was no doubt a naturalist and one of the first to appreciate the beauty and wonder of our county.

As John's children grew up and married, they left the area, and all seemed well. Then suddenly, his young wife died, leaving him a middle-aged widower. John sold the family home and moved into a small cabin on the Kiel road, which is today the main entrance to the marsh.

The area around John's cabin soon became a jumble of rocks, odd-shaped roots, Indian artifacts and anything else that he was interested in. The inside of his home many would consider intolerably cluttered. Stacks of books and magazines, some nearly one hundred years old, notebooks and papers were piled nearly to the ceiling; only narrow paths were left for him to walk through. What other people considered clutter was, to him, his library and a lifetime of collections.

Even though John sought a solitary life, he was by no means a hermit. His door was always open to visitors. With his frequent visits to the Elkhart area, he became very well known. For guests at nearby resorts, it was an absolute must to make a visit to the old man at his cabin and chat with him, which he always enjoyed. John had let his snowy white hair grow, which by then reached down to his shoulders. He once said he hadn't had a haircut in twenty-five years.

A rumor began to circulate that Sexton was very wealthy and had a large sum of cash hidden in his small cabin. One of the people who heard and apparently believed the rumor was a recent Italian immigrant, Anthony Borello. Borello worked in the nearby Rhine Mills limestone quarry near John's home. It was while working in the quarry that Borello heard the rumor of the hoard of cash Sexton allegedly kept in his cabin.

On the night of June 28, 1911, Borello entered Sexton's home with the intent to rob him. Evidence at the crime scene indicated that John had put up a terrific struggle in defense of his life. The following day, the body of eighty-eight-year-old John L. Sexton was found in his cabin, brutally murdered. The victim was stabbed many times, and his throat was slit from ear to ear.

After an extensive investigation, it was felt that the murderer was Anthony Borello, who it was learned had fled back to his homeland of Italy. Italian authorities were contacted by the Sheboygan County Sheriff's Department, and they were able to locate, arrest and hold him for American law enforcement officers. A sheriff's deputy and a detective from the Sheboygan Police Department journeyed to Italy, a trip that took several months, to pick up Borello and return him to Sheboygan County for trial. However, once the U.S. officers arrived in Italy, the Italian authorities refused to release the accused murderer. The Italian judiciary felt that Borello might not get a fair trial in the United States. Borello was then charged with the murder of John Sexton and tried in an Italian court. After a lengthy trial, Borello was found guilty and sentenced to seventeen years in prison.

During the trial, it was brought out that the total amount of cash Borello found in John Sexton's cabin was less than $300, the old man's entire life savings.

Murder in a "Soft Drink Parlor"

Prohibition, which prohibited the manufacture, sale, barter, transport, export, delivery or furnishing of intoxicating beverages, was a constitutional amendment that had been in effect since January 1920. Also known as the Volstead Act or the Eighteenth Amendment, it was the most ill thought out and flagrantly violated law in the history of our country.

The government created a force of only 1,500 federal agents to police the entire country and enforce an extremely unpopular law that many of the agents did not agree with. A force so small was totally incapable of stemming the flood of illicit liquor and beer from illegal stills all over the country. Even local law enforcement often turned a blind eye to saloons that were operating openly. Sheboygan was no exception.

Prior to the start of Prohibition, the city directory listed over 120 taverns; after Prohibition, the city directory listed 120 "soft drink and ice cream parlors." The so-called soft drink parlors operated openly with little fear of prosecution. It didn't take long for the criminal element in our country to step forward to supply the unquenchable thirst of a nation of lawbreakers, and in so doing reaped enormous profits.

In one of the most corrupt cities of the era, Chicago, gangland wars raged across the city. Mobster gangs competed with one another over rights to distribute illicit alcohol in certain areas of the city. Murders were a commonplace event; a mostly corrupt police force took little action to bring the turf wars to a halt.

Nearly every day, newspapers across the country printed lurid photos of mobsters sprawled in pools of blood in the streets of Chicago after having been gunned down by a rival gang. The favored weapon was the Thompson .45-caliber submachine gun. The Thompson often was carried in a violin case and was nicknamed the "Chicago Piano" or the "Chicago Typewriter."

In Sheboygan, residents read the stories of Chicago mob wars, bloody shootouts, corrupt officials and gangsters who became rich overnight with little concern. They were after all insulated from all that by being over 150 miles away from the chaos.

Passersby today take little notice of a small, white, nondescript building located at 1219 Broadway Avenue. Built in 1890, the shabby little structure today gives no hint that at one time it was the scene of a brutal and senseless murder. At the time of the murder, the building was known as Otto Kohls Saloon. The business, operated by Kohls for many years, was well known around the city, and Otto himself was a well-respected businessman. When the murder took place in his saloon on that fateful March 19, 1927, Prohibition had already been in effect for seven years. It might be noted that everyone who lived on the south side of Sheboygan euphemistically referred to it as Otto Kohls Soft Drink Parlor.

At about 12:10 a.m. on the day in question, Kohls related that he had seven patrons at the bar sipping root beer while he began cleaning up the saloon (correction: soda parlor) in preparation to close at 1:00 a.m. As Otto began sweeping the floor, two young men entered the saloon, both of them strangers. It was not unusual for complete strangers to enter the bar, as it was located just about a block east of Highway 17, which at that time was the main road to Milwaukee and ran along the present-day Business Drive.

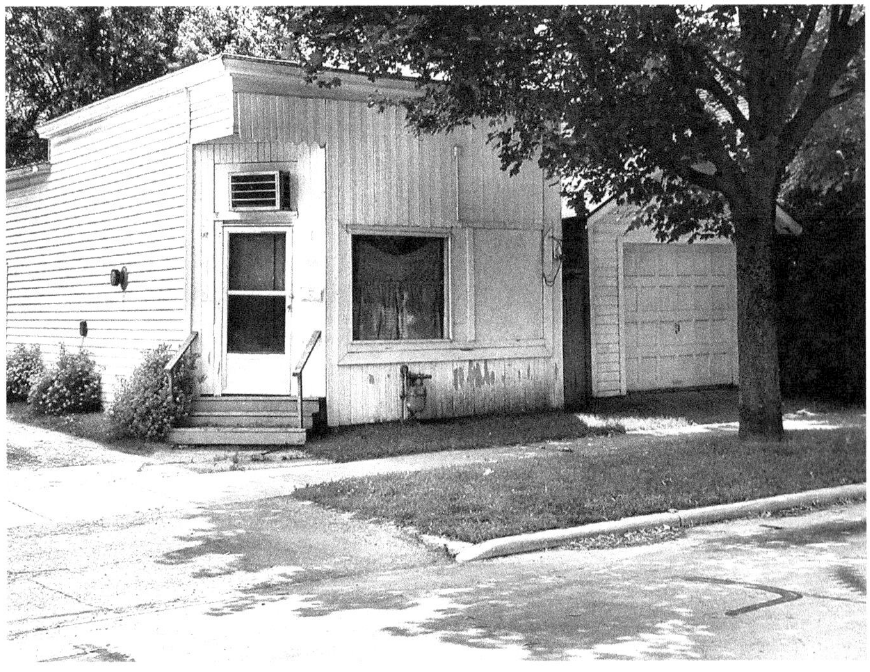

Scene of the 1927 Jonassen murder at 1219 Broadway, as it appears today. The building has changed little since 1927. *Photo by the author.*

The first man inquired as to where the men's room was located and was directed to the back of the barroom by Kohls. The second stranger stayed at the end of the bar closest to the front door and purchased a pack of cigarettes. Suddenly, the first man reappeared at the back of the barroom and shouted, "This is a stickup, get your hands in the air." The startled patrons whirled around toward the rear of the tavern and observed the young man menacingly brandishing two handguns. The stranger near the front of the bar also drew a gun from his pocket. He then ordered Kohls and his patrons to line up against the east wall of the tavern. Once all the patrons were being held against the wall, the first gunman went behind the bar and emptied the cash register of $115.

Coming out from behind the bar, the young thug held the frightened customers at bay while he ordered them to empty the contents of their pockets into his hat. As the two-gun bandit went down the line of terrified victims one by one, the customers complied with the thieves' order to turn over all their cash and personal possessions. As ordered, rings, watches, several pocketknives and cash were dumped into the young robber's hat.

Everyone cooperated quickly with the robbers except one. Thirty-six-year-old Olaf I. Jonassen, who was described as a rather large and very strong man, apparently decided he was not about to give up his hard-earned cash or valuables to a couple of cocky young thieves.

As the two-gun bandit approached, Olaf, seeing an opportunity, startled the bar patrons as well as the would-be thief by suddenly lunging at him. The force of Olaf hitting the holdup man carried them backward and down to the floor. For several moments, unbelieving witnesses watched as Olaf struggled with the smaller man. At one point, it seemed that Olaf would prevail. The first young thief still standing at the front of the barroom pointed his gun toward Kohls and ordered him to pull Olaf off his partner. Kohls refused, fearing he might get shot in the melee by the second holdup man who was still holding on to his two guns. Suddenly, the roar of a gun being discharged was heard by the frightened patrons. Olaf stopped struggling, and his body went limp, jolting the startled patrons. The furious criminal jumped to his feet and began pumping bullets into the helpless wounded man already lying in a pool of blood. Then his partner ran up to the victim and began shooting into Olaf's body. During a later investigation, it was learned that eleven shots had been fired, eight of which struck Olaf, three of them in his head.

The brutal killers then grabbed their loot and frantically fled from the building to their car, which had been left standing at the curb, motor running. When last seen, the bandits were fleeing south on Highway 17 at a high rate of speed. Patrons of the bar rushed to Olaf's side; he lay facedown in an ever-widening pool of blood.

Then one of the patrons remembered that a doctor lived close by. He ran to the doctor's home and managed to wake him up. Upon learning of the shooting, the doctor hurried to Kohls's saloon. After a brief examination of the lifeless body of Olaf, the doctor sadly shook his head. Olaf Jonassen was dead.

Blue wisps of gun smoke and the acrid smell of burnt gunpowder filled the air of Otto Kohls's saloon as police officers arrived. As the first two officers entered the crime scene, they were confronted with patrons who were still in stunned disbelief, trying to comprehend the cold-blooded murder they had just witnessed. Realizing they were on a major crime scene, the officers called headquarters and asked for detectives and additional officers to assist in the investigation. The coroner was summoned, as well as the chief of police. Soon the tiny saloon was filled with grim-faced investigators.

When the cruel young thieves killed Olaf Jonassen, they had no idea that they were depriving the elderly parents of the victim of their sole means of support. Mr. and Mrs. Ole Jonassen had little in the way of financial resources and depended entirely on their bachelor son, Olaf, who lived with them and provided them with their day-to-day needs. Also living in the Jonassen home at the time was eight-year-old Harold Nelson, who happened to be visiting his grandparents at the time. When I spoke to the elderly Nelson many years later, he said that he clearly remembered the night his uncle was murdered.

The following is a brief but poignant statement written about the old man's recollections of that terrible night:

> *At the time of my Uncle's death, I was staying at my grandmother's house in Sheboygan. I woke up late at night and the house was full of people whispering to each other. At the time I had no idea what was going on. Later on I remember Doc, that was my Uncle Olaf's nickname, laid out in a coffin in the front room of our home. Looking into the coffin I counted the holes in his head filled with something similar to wax.*

The statement was signed Harold Nelson, July 15, 2000.

Now the investigation began in earnest. Descriptions of the armed bandits were given out by phone to all police agencies in the area. The chief of police ordered that police motorcycles equipped with sidecars and manned by two officers be sent north on Highway 17 toward Manitowoc and west on Highway 23 toward Plymouth. Chief of Police Wagner and Detectives Hermann and Rothe took a detective car and headed south toward Milwaukee on Highway 17 to search for the murderers. The Sheboygan officers drove all the way to Milwaukee without sighting the alleged murderers. Once at Milwaukee, Chief Wagner went to the central police station, where he gave them a complete description of the two men and the car that the authorities were looking for. Milwaukee authorities informed Chief Wagner that they already had in custody, on another matter, two men who seemed to fit the description the chief had just given them. The chief then called Sheboygan and asked that Otto Kohls be brought to Milwaukee as soon as possible for a possible identification of the two suspects held by Milwaukee police. A few hours later, Otto Kohls arrived at the Milwaukee Police Department, and officers there arranged a lineup. Much to the disappointment of everyone, Kohls was unable to identify anyone in the lineup. The chief then drove on to Chicago to confer with authorities there.

The next day, the car used in the robbery was found mired down on a muddy side road in the Black River area just south of Sheboygan. A check of the license plates showed that the car had been stolen from the city of

Manitowoc several days earlier. Sheriff's deputies found bloodstains in the car, along with some of the personal items that the holdup men had taken during the robbery of the victims and then discarded. Sheriff's officers then searched summer cottages in the immediate area and found one that had been broken into. Apparently, the gunmen had spent the night in the secluded cabin. After that the trail went cold—the murderers had escaped.

One piece of evidence investigating officers had was the stolen car that had apparently been driven by the killers. Investigators felt that the two escaped thieves had to have some connection in the Manitowoc area; otherwise why would they have been in Manitowoc?

Manitowoc officers began to scour their records looking for any known local criminals who might fit the description of the two murderers. A theory was developing that possibly the wanted men were from the Manitowoc area. A few days after the murder in Sheboygan, which by now had received widespread media coverage, a tip was received from a Manitowoc merchant. The merchant said that a customer had brought in a coat of the type that had been worn by one of Jonassen's killers. The merchant said that the coat had several dark stains on it that he assumed was dried blood. A label inside the coat indicated that it was owned by Albert Lutzke, who was known to area police. The physical description of Lutzke somewhat fit the description of one of Jonassen's murderers.

A pickup order was put out on Lutzke, and Manitowoc authorities scoured the county looking for the suspect. The coat was turned over to Sheboygan Police, who sent it to a laboratory to try and determine the blood type. Manitowoc County sheriff's investigators received information on where they might locate the elusive Lutzke. Officers were directed to a farm that was owned by an associate of his. When the farm owner was asked if he knew where Lutzke might be, he claimed he hadn't seen him for some time. Dubious officers began to search the property. As the searcher entered the farm home, they carefully searched the house room by room and finally located Lutzke hiding under a bed.

Police Chief Wagner was contacted, and he was informed that a suspect in the Jonassen murder was being held in the Manitowoc County Jail. The chief picked up several of the witnesses to the murder and drove to Manitowoc for a lineup. Again, much to the disappointment of law officers, the witnesses were unable to identify the suspect Lutzke. However, while Lutzke was being held, it was discovered that there were several outstanding warrants on him.

The people of Sheboygan were shocked and appalled by the brutality of the attack that ended in the death of the unfortunate bar patron. As the days since the murder passed, pressure on the Sheboygan Police to effect an arrest increased. After all, things like this just did not happen in Sheboygan. They wanted the guilty parties apprehended and brought to trial, now! The angry citizens of Sheboygan had no idea just how long this would take.

Sheboygan Mayor L.E. Larson stepped forward and made an extraordinary proposal to the common council. He proposed that the City of Sheboygan, during these hard times, offer a $500 (in today's money $6,200) reward for the arrest and conviction of the murderers of Olaf Jonassen. A resolution was drafted and passed almost without debate. The reward offer brought forth several tips, all of them false. The investigation was stalled, and investigators had hit a brick wall. It began to look as though the killers would never be caught. Almost one month to the day after the murder, an event took place 250 miles south of Sheboygan in the state of Illinois that would change all that.

On April 18, 1927, an event occurred that would have a significant effect on the Jonassen murder. On that early spring day, twenty-one-year-old Arthur Goetzke, an employee of Bolden's shoe store in downtown Bloomington, Illinois, had just opened the store for the day when he noticed two men peering in the window. Thinking they were perspective customers, Arthur walked to the front of the store. As the two men entered, one of them stopped near the door and the other walked toward the rear of the store. Arthur inquired politely, "May I help you gentlemen?" The young clerk was then startled to hear a gruff voice behind him order, "Turn around." When Arthur turned around, he found himself staring down the barrel of a gun. The gunman growled, "This is a stickup, get in the back of the store." With a gun barrel jabbing him in the back, the terrified young man was herded into the back room, which was separated from the main store by a curtain. Once in the back of the store, the would-be robbers ordered Arthur to open the store safe. The trembling clerk stammered, "I can't open the safe, I don't have the combination." Jamming the barrel of his gun under Arthur's chin, the thug demanded to know who had the combination. Arthur, his mouth so dry he could barely speak, said in a trembling voice, "Only Mr. Bolden has the combination." "And when does he get here?" demanded the holdup man, who was now getting impatient. "Soon," Arthur mumbled. All the while Arthur was being interrogated by the gun-toting thief, his partner kept casting furtive glances from behind the curtain toward the front of the store.

With Arthur being held captive in the rear of the store, the other bandit moved out from behind the curtain and took up a position near the front door. Before long, the store owner, Mr. Ernest L. Bolden, entered his store, only to

$500 REWARD $500

For Information Leading To The Arrest

Wanted FOR MURDER And Hold-Up

On the morning of March 19th, at 12:15 A. M., the soft drink parlor of Otto Kohls, this city, was held up by the following described suspects, who shot and killed Olaf Jonassen, one of the occupants in said place of business.

DESCRIPTION OF SUBJECTS

NO. 1—Age 25 to 28 years. 5 ft. 5 or 6 in. tall. Weight 135 to 145 lbs. Slightly cross-eyed, dark complexion, looks like an Italian, wore dark blue suit, gray hat, no overcoat, fairly well dressed, carried and used two automatic pistols (32 caliber).

NO. 2—Age 23 to 27 years. 5 ft. 7 or 8 in. tall. Weight 135 to 145 lbs., very slim build, light or sandy complexion, wore powder blue or dark gray overcoat and gray cap, carried and used nickel plated pistol (32 caliber).

Kindly be on lookout for these subjects. Hold any suspicious looking characters and notify the undersigned. Will be able to identify.

WALTER H. WAGNER,
Chief of Police,
Sheboygan, Wisconsin.

After the murder, wanted posters were distributed throughout the Midwest by Sheboygan Police. *Author's collection.*

have a gun thrust up against his head and be ordered to the back of the store. Under the threat of death, Bolden, with trembling hands, opened the safe. The thieves then snatched $430 in cash and $35 in checks from the safe and ordered both men to lie on the floor. One of the robbers had stepped out of the back room and returned quickly with several pairs of silk stockings, which they used to tie up their captives. The gunmen then fled out the front door and into a car that had been parked in front of the store with the motor running.

It was later learned that as soon as the bandits left the Bolden shoe store, Mr. Bolden and his clerk were able to free themselves and call police. Witnesses on the street pointed out to the officers the direction the robbers had fled only moments before and gave police a description of the getaway car. The witnesses further told the investigating officers that the getaway car was last seen traveling north on North Main Street at a high rate of speed. As the car driven by the robbers sped down the street in an attempt to escape, it very nearly missed a collision with a car driven by William Smith with his three children, which almost forced them off the road. The robbers were unaware that just a few blocks down the street, North Main Street was closed to traffic because of high water from a rainstorm the night before that had flooded the roadway near a subway entrance. Angrily, Smith turned his car around so as to pursue the reckless driver who had nearly struck him and his family. He had gone no more than a block when he saw the car he was after stalled in a large pool of water beneath a viaduct. Smith then stopped his car and asked his thirteen-year-old son to run over to the car and get the license number so they could report it to police. The bandits, however, noticed the boy behind them and became suspicious of his interest in their car. Putting the car in gear, the thieves began turning over the engine with the starter, which caused the car to move ahead out of the pool of water. The two robbers then jumped out of their car, continued their flight on foot and disappeared. At this time, the Smith family was in the little village of Norman, which is just immediately north of Bloomington. Smith ran to a grocery store and called the Norman Police, informing them of the incident with the recklessly driven car, and advised them that he thought possibly the car was stolen. Smith was still not aware that the car and its occupants were wanted by Bloomington Police for armed robbery.

The Norman Police and all surrounding police departments in the area had been advised to watch all highways in their area and to be alert for any strangers they might encounter. When Smith told the Norman Police about the car he had trouble with, they immediately realized that it could, most likely, be the car that law enforcement agencies were looking for.

As soon as word was given out that the fugitive car was in Norman, the area was flooded with police officers from every jurisdiction nearby. As the manhunt went on, officers received information that two suspicious-looking men had been seen walking along a nearby railroad track. The chief of police from Norman and a detective began walking along the train tracks looking for the bandits. As they searched down the tracks, they saw a large German shepherd dog excitedly running around a clump of grapevines. The dog ran up to the two officers and then turned and ran back to the grapevines. He did this several times, leaving officers to believe there was something in the tangle of vines that the dog wanted them to see. Suddenly, investigators saw a movement in the clump of vines, then a head popped up and they were able to see someone in the hiding place draw what appeared to be a gun. The officers dropped to the ground and ordered whoever was in the brush to come out with their hands up. Much to their surprise, the bandits surrendered immediately and meekly crawled out of their hiding place. Officers quickly placed the two suspects in handcuffs, and both were searched by arresting officers. During the search, investigators found that one of the suspects was carrying two guns. One was a .25 caliber automatic and the other was a .32-caliber automatic. The second suspect was armed with a .38-caliber revolver. They also recovered most, but not all, of the loot from the shoe store robbery. They then marched them out to a nearby road, where they were picked up and taken to the Bloomington city jail and interrogated by detectives.

The two men were identified as Andrew Young and Frank Allgood, both of Springfield, Illinois. As detectives began their interrogation of the two men, they suddenly realized that their descriptions and the weapons they were carrying were remarkably similar to those listed on a wanted poster pertaining to a murder in Sheboygan, Wisconsin. A phone call was placed to Sheboygan Police Chief Walter Wagner, who agreed with Bloomington detectives that the two men being held by them could possibly be the killers of Olaf Jonassen.

Chief Wagner, Otto Kohls and Roland Marten, one of the patrons who had been in the bar when the murder took place, immediately drove to Bloomington, Illinois, for possible identification. Bloomington officers were going to immediately arrange a lineup but postponed it until the following morning. It was decided that the witnesses from Sheboygan would stand in a darkened corridor as the jail prisoners filed by for breakfast to see if they could identify anyone. Kohls and the other murder witnesses had been advised by authorities that if they recognized anyone they were to say nothing and show no sign of recognition. With Chief Wagner and a detective watching the two witnesses, they suddenly saw Kohls and Marten stiffen as the prisoners shuffled by. Once the prisoners had passed them and were seated in a large dining hall, Kohls and Marten were taken to a secluded area where they could get a better look at the men. Both of them had no difficulty picking out Young and Allgood as the murderers.

Both Allgood and Young were immediately taken out of the breakfast hall and placed in separate cells so that they could be interrogated by Chief Wagner. After a lengthy questioning session, the chief did obtain confessions, but not the ones he wanted. Both Allgood and Young confessed to the armed robbery in Bloomington but stoutly maintained they knew absolutely nothing about the murder in Sheboygan. But the evidence against the two began to pile up. First, there was the positive identification by two witnesses; secondly there were the three guns that were of exactly the same type and caliber as the murder weapons. Then there was a small pocketknife that was found in Allgood's pocket. It was identified by Marten as being the one that was taken from him the night of the murder. It seemed as though Sheboygan had an airtight case and the murder of Jonassen was at last solved.

Chief Wagner had the Sheboygan district attorney draw up warrants for murder in the first degree against Young and Allgood. It was the chief's intention to serve the warrants and then transport the suspects back to Sheboygan for trial. Much to the chief's astonishment, Illinois authorities blocked this move. The Bloomington district attorney insisted that the men be tried first in Illinois for armed robbery, but he further assured Wisconsin authorities that when the two men were tried and sent to jail, Wisconsin would be notified when their sentences had been served. Both Young and Allgood were then held in the county jail for trial in lieu of a $5,000 bond, which they could not post.

While the two men were awaiting trial, it was discovered that both of them had fairly lengthy criminal records and had already served time in prison. Toward the end of 1927, the two gunmen stood trial in Illinois and were found guilty and sentenced to ten years to life at hard labor in the Illinois state prison at Joliet. Sheboygan would just have to wait until the two criminals were released to prosecute them. Twelve years passed by, and in November 1939, Young was released to Sheboygan authorities for trial. Allgood, however, had not yet completed his sentence and was still being held in Illinois.

After twelve long years, the murder trial of Andrew Young was about to begin. Young had procured the services of Jacob J. Fessler and Arthur

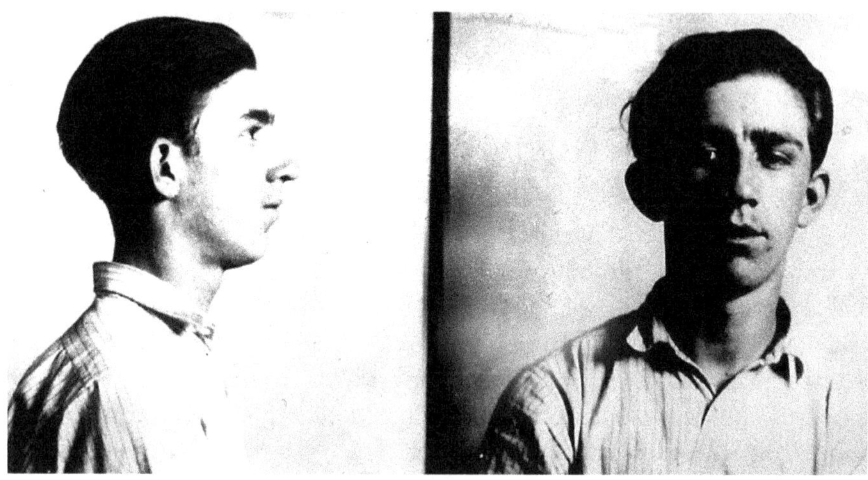

A mug shot of suspected murderer Andrew Young, taken by Illinois authorities. *Author's collection.* Author's note: No photograph of Frank Allgood could be located.

Grube, considered by many to be two of the best attorneys in Sheboygan. Prior to the start of the trial, Attorney Fessler had gone to the Illinois state prison and had taken a deposition from Frank Allgood. It was during the taking of this deposition that Allgood admitted his guilt in the shooting of Jonassen and swore that Andrew Young was not the person who was with him during the robbery and murder. In fact, Allgood swore the man with him was a criminal from Illinois known as "Short Arm Louie," whose name was Louis Schomber. Schomber did in some ways resemble Andrew Young. Unfortunately, or maybe fortunately, Schomber was deceased. Attorney Fessler also filed a notice of alibi stating on the day in question Andrew Young was not in the city of Sheboygan or even in the state of Wisconsin.

At last, the trial of Young was set for December 22, 1939, at 8:00 a.m. The problem the state was having was that after twelve years, the memories of the witnesses had dimmed, including Chief of Police Wagner, who on several occasions contradicted himself. But much to the distress of the defense, witness after witness took the stand and swore that Andrew Young was the murderer. After five days of testimony, during which the defense claimed that Young was a victim of mistaken identity, the trial came to an end. After deliberating only five hours, the jury came in with a verdict. The presiding judge postponed the reading of the verdict until 9:00 a.m. the following day. The next day, the courtroom was packed with spectators, including the family of Andrew Young. The jury handed their verdict to the judge, who asked

Young to stand and face the bench. The verdict was guilty of murder in the first degree. Young's family wept quietly. Sentencing was set for December 29, 1939, at which time Judge Detling sentenced Young to life in prison.

Andrew Young always maintained his innocence even after his incarceration. Young appealed his case in the appellate courts and the state supreme court, all to no avail. In 1942, he filed an application for executive clemency with Governor Julius Heil but was turned down. It seemed that Andrew Young was destined to spend the rest of his life behind bars.

Andrew Young would not take no for an answer, continually insisting that he was innocent. According to old court records, Young again applied for executive clemency on September 10, 1943, to the new governor, Walter Goodland. Again he was turned down. On February 10, 1944, he again failed to gain release from prison. In 1945, he filed another appeal, and this time it was granted. Records indicate that prior to his release it was learned that a new drug, sodium amatol, commonly known as truth serum, had been administered to him with Young's permission. This procedure was conducted in a hospital in the presence of two competent psychiatrists. While in an induced state of narcosis, Young was questioned at length and in great detail. Also present at this time was a special investigator from the governor's office. The investigator who conducted the questioning stated that he could not change Young's claim of innocence.

Because of this and because Young had shown a remarkable record of rehabilitation in prison, the pardon was granted. The trial judge, Henry Detling, wrote a letter to Governor Goodland protesting the pardon; however, the governor declined to change his decision.

Having read in the news of the controversial decision, the circuit court judge of the Tenth Judicial Circuit wrote a letter to Judge Detling stating that he also had experience with the so-called truth serum and stated that he would shortly be sending him a letter explaining his experiences. The letter to Judge Detling was signed by the circuit court judge, Joseph R. McCarthy, who would shortly become Wisconsin's infamous Senator McCarthy.

On January 4, 1946, prisoner #25321 walked out of Waupon State Prison a free man. The new Wisconsin governor, Walter S. Goodland, had granted Andrew Young a full and complete pardon.

What became of Frank Allgood? In July 1941, he was brought to Wisconsin for trial. On August 21, 1941, Allgood pled guilty to a reduced charge of second-degree murder and was sentenced to fourteen to twenty-five years in prison. In 1949, Frank Allgood was paroled after serving eight years in prison for the murder of Olaf Jonassen.

It might be noted that when Andrew Young was found guilty of first-degree murder in 1939, he was the first person in the history of Sheboygan County to have been found guilty of murder in the first degree.

A VISIT TO THE NEIGHBORS

When the first settlers arrived in Sheboygan County, they found a wilderness almost beyond comprehension. In many places, the forests were so dense that a horse could not be ridden through it. These early settlers found life in our area filled with danger and hardships. The forest itself presented a dark, mysterious and fearful presence of a thousand terrors, some real and others imagined. The natives who lived in the area were a peaceful lot, but could they be trusted? After all, they were forest creatures themselves and part of the settlers' darkest fears.

It was not uncommon for early residents of the county to become lost and disoriented one hundred yards from home. Many homes had a large brass horn hanging over the fireplace that was used to signal to family members lost in the woods. If someone went off to pick berries or hunt and did not return home on time, the horn was brought out and a long blast on the horn was blown, hopefully steering the lost person to the safety of home and hearth. Getting lost in the dense forest was not the only peril the pioneers faced. There were also the vicious packs of wolves that roamed the area. Early farmers had to build high, secure board fences around any animals they kept. Cattle, pigs and chickens were all favorite meals for the ever-hungry wolves. One settler had a two-hundred-pound mastiff dog to protect his property; a pack of wolves had no trouble killing him.

In the year 1846, a family's worst fears became reality. J.W. Briggs, his wife Asenath and their children purchased a small tract of wilderness land near what was to become the city of Plymouth. After countless hours of backbreaking labor, Briggs managed to hack a small clearing out of the dense forest and put up a log cabin for his family, with the assistance of neighbors. The task of clearing land and putting up a cabin was so arduous that one man could never have done it alone. People needed each other's help just to survive. If a farmer was taken sick at harvest time, settlers from miles around brought in the crops without ever being asked. Tools and draft animals were freely borrowed back and forth. Women thought nothing of walking miles along forest trails to help out a neighbor lady who just had a baby or was injured or ill. In fact, the pioneer women were happy to be able

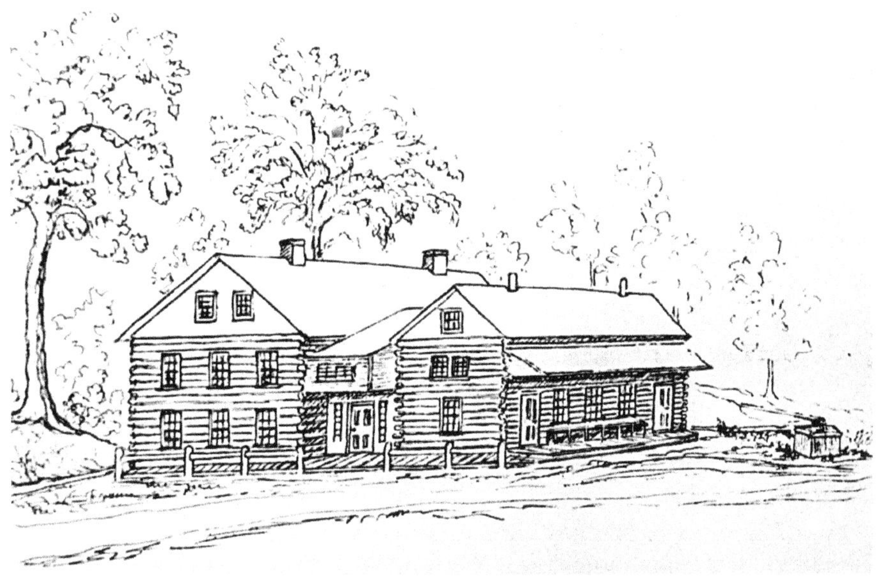

Cold spring house, one of the earliest buildings in the Plymouth area, as it appeared about the time Mrs. Briggs was murdered. *Courtesy Sheboygan County Historic Research Center.*

to meet with other women and break the lonely and tedious routine they daily faced.

Early in the morning May 16, Asenath Briggs was about to bake bread when she found that she was short of flour and milk. Picking up a pail and a measure, she wrapped her shawl over her shoulders and informed her husband that she was going to the neighbor's house, less than a half mile away, to borrow the needed ingredients and would not be gone long because she was anxious to start her baking.

The trail through the dark forest that she took was one that Mrs. Briggs knew well and had walked many times. The trail did, however, pass through one of the darkest and densest parts of the woods.

After hours passed, Mr. Briggs became alarmed when his wife did not return home. Thinking that perhaps she had had an accident and might be lying along the trail to the neighbor's house, he set out to look for her. Briggs walked all the way to his neighbors' house without seeing a sign of his missing wife. When he contacted the neighbors, they told him that his wife had never arrived. The astonished man realized that something serious must have happened to her. Somewhere along the dark, forbidding trail, Asenath Briggs had vanished!

The call for a search party went out, and men from miles around dropped what they were doing and assembled at the Briggs farm, many of them armed. The searchers fanned out in every direction. For hours, they tramped the heavily wooded area, crashed through underbrush and waded across creeks and through swamps—but not a trace of the missing woman could be found. As darkness settled over them, the searchers quit for the night, only to go out again the next day. After several days, the quest to find the missing farm wife was deemed hopeless, and the horrible truth became apparent: Mrs. Briggs was gone.

Weeks passed, and then a report was received from local Indians that they had found the body of a white woman in Manitowoc County near the Sheboygan River at a site known to them as Big Bend, which was over twenty miles away. Briggs, along with several neighbors, quickly set out for the location of the corpse the Indians said they found.

When Briggs and his neighbors arrived, they were not quite prepared for what they found. The body was positively identified as the missing Mrs. Briggs. She lay on her shawl; all her clothes had been removed and were found lying on top of her. Nearby lay the pail and the measure she left home with. Most gruesome of all was the fact that her head had been removed from her torso and was lying next to her!

Many questions remained and still do: how did the victim end up at a spot more than twenty miles from home in a place she had no reason to be? How did Asenath Briggs die? Who or what killed her? Her mysterious death remains unsolved to this day.

Asenath Briggs's strange disappearance and her eventual murder is only one of many strange happenings that have taken place in the Sheboygan area.

CHAPTER 3
TALES OF MYSTERY

WHAT EVER HAPPENED TO RAY?

On March 18, 1940, an event occurred in Sheboygan that involved the Sheboygan Police Department in one of the strangest and most bizarre cases they ever handled, even to this day. It seems that the more they investigated and the more facts they gathered, the less they really understood what actually took place in the basement boiler room of the First Congregational Church on that that fateful day. After an intensive investigation, many questions were left unanswered, and the mystery of what ever happened to Ray remains just that—a mystery

Every city and town has people like Ray. Many of them are of diminished mental capacity and live on the edges of society. We see them every day but never really see them; they are almost invisible. Most of these invisible persons can, and do, function; some are able to support themselves by working at menial jobs. Ray Colbath was just such an invisible man. Ray was familiar to almost everybody who lived or worked in the downtown area of Sheboygan, but very few knew his name or anything about him.

Ray Colbath, age thirty, was a quiet, gentle, almost reclusive man. His life was simple but well ordered. He was very punctual, polite and a hard worker. He was unmarried and had few possessions, few friends and almost certainly no enemies… that anybody knew of. His most treasured possession was his shiny new Schwinn bicycle. Ray had saved enough from his meager income to buy the bike of his dreams. The bike had a knee action fork, a tank on the center frame and a light and horn mounted on the front. To this, Ray added white handlebar grips with plastic multicolored streamers attached to the end of the grips. On days when he was not working, he was a familiar sight on Eighth Street, where he could be seen, with streamers flying, pedaling as fast as he could through downtown traffic. At night before he put his bike away, he would wipe it all down with loving care and put his treasured vehicle in the front vestibule of his sister's home. Most certainly he never took his treasured bike out on a rainy day.

Ray lived quietly with his sister and brother-in-law, Mr. and Mrs. Erv Schienle, in the 1700 block of North Second Street. Mornings he could be found working as a part-time janitor at the YMCA, which in those days was located at 713 Ontario Avenue. Ray worked at the Y from 8:00 a.m. until noon, when he would go home to have lunch with his sister. At precisely 1:00 p.m., he would appear at the First Congregational Church, which was just around the corner from the YMCA and was located at 926 North Seventh Street, where he also worked as a part-time custodian several days a week from 1:00 p.m. to 5:00 p.m. Then he would go home and have an almost silent dinner with his sister and brother-in-law. After dinner, he would retire to his room and listen to his radio until 9:00 p.m., which was bedtime. With no variation, the days passed by quietly for Ray. For most of us, the maddening routine would be all but unbearable, but Ray found comfort in

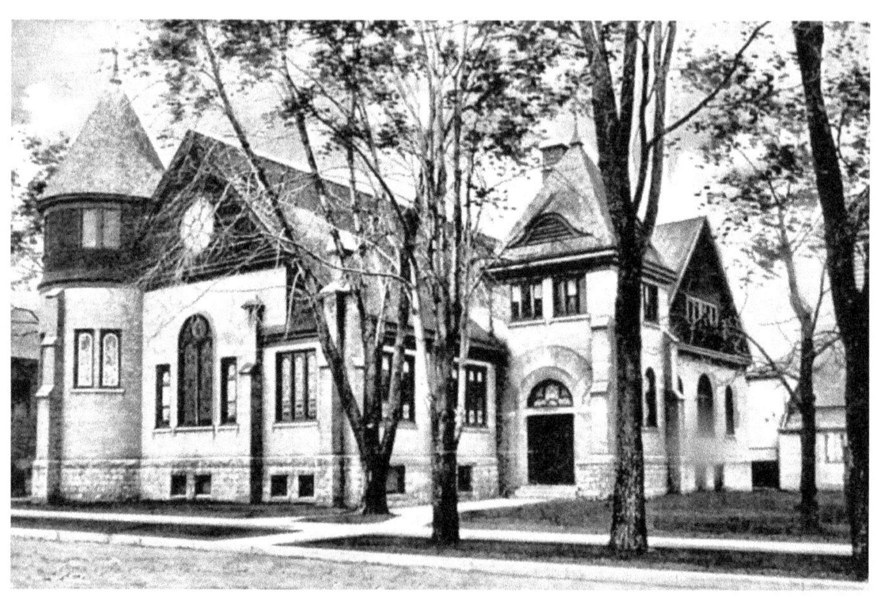

The First Congregational Church, the scene of Ray's death. *Author's collection.*

his strictly regulated life. March 19, 1940, was to be a vastly different day for the quiet, soft-spoken man.

On this day, Ray was late for dinner, and almost immediately his sister became concerned. Normally if a thirty-year-old man is a few minutes late for dinner it would be of no cause for concern, but Ray was never late for dinner, especially when he knew they were having pot roast, his favorite meal. The minutes and then the hours slowly ticked by. By the time the clock reached midnight, Ray's sister was frantic. She begged her husband Erv to go out and look for her missing brother. It was a cold, damp, windy night, and Erv reluctantly pulled on his coat and began walking toward the place Ray would have last been: the First Congregational Church.

As Erv approached the church, he noted that there were several lights burning inside, so he tried the front door, and it was locked. Going around to the side door, Erv saw Ray's treasured bike with a bicycle lock in place as usual. This meant that his missing brother-in-law was surely inside. Trying the side door, he found it open, and once inside, he loudly called out Ray's name, his voice echoing through the empty church, but received no response. He called out again, but the silence was broken only by the hollow sound of his own footsteps on the tile floor. By now Erv began to fear the worst; had his brother-in-law suffered a serious accident and was lying injured somewhere in the cavernous building? Or worse, was he dead? Erv checked the main floor of the church and then the pastor's office; all was in order. He then climbed the stairs to the choir loft; it, too, was empty. This left the basement. Ray had to be down there. He would never have left the building with the lights on and the door unlocked. And then there was his bike. It was unthinkable that he would have left and not taken his bike with him. Erv entered the basement church hall. Here, too, the lights were on. Ray also detected the strong smell of cleaning solutions that had been used to mop the freshly scrubbed floors, but other than that the room was empty. This left only four small rooms: the men's and ladies' restrooms, a storage room where tables and chairs were kept and the boiler room. Erv methodically checked the restrooms, and again the smell of cleaning products greeted his nostrils in the recently sanitized rooms; both were dark and empty. The storage room was likewise empty; this left only the boiler room. The boiler room door was a heavy metal fireproof door to which a chain was attached. The chain was connected to a weight that would drop if there were a fire and slam the door shut if it were open. All the while that Erv was in the church, he thought that even though it was a nasty, cold, windy night it was unusually warm in the building. Erv would very soon find out the reason for this.

Gingerly, Erv pushed the heavy door open, the chain rattling through a pulley near the top of the door. Erv knew that Ray had to be in this room. With his heart pounding, he swung the door wide open and was startled by a tremendous blast of heat and an almost white light of great intensity nearly blinding him. Erv stopped dead in his tracks as he stared at the boiler. His mind was totally incapable of accepting the scene before him. The bewildered man staggered back and in sheer terror and horror ran from the boiler room, the heavy door slamming shut behind him.

It had been a quiet night at the Sheboygan Police Department. The shift commander had a difficult time keeping awake, and then the phone rang. Picking up the phone, he announced in a monotone, "Sheboygan Police Department." Instantly, a male began screaming, "Come quick, hurry, hurry it's awful!" "Where are you?" the puzzled officer, now wide awake, asked. "The church, the church," the caller stammered. "What church?" the officer asked. "The First Congregational Church, and hurry," he said and hung up. A patrol car was immediately dispatched and, not knowing just what was happening, another was sent for backup.

When the officers arrived, they found a man in front of the church in a state of great agitation, nearly incoherent. After a few moments, they were able to calm him down enough to identify himself as Erv Schienle. Between sobs and gasps, the distraught witness told the officers what he had seen in the boiler room. The two seasoned veterans stared at each other in disbelief. Quickly they entered the church and rushed to the basement boiler room. With no small amount of trepidation, they slowly pushed the heavy metal door open and were almost overcome by the blast of heat and the intense light. A police officer during his career is exposed to many unpleasant sights, but nothing could have prepared them for what they saw. Sticking out of the open boiler door was a pair of human legs that were bare except the feet had socks and shoes on them. The remains were apparently those of a male, but nothing above the upper thigh existed. The rest of the body had been consumed in the roaring flames. On the floor lay a pile of men's clothing.

One of the officers sent a hurried call for help to headquarters, requested a supervisor and gave a brief report of the situation in the boiler room of the church basement. Within a very short time, investigators swarmed over the church. Due to the extreme overheating of the heavily stoked furnace, the fire department was called to stand by in case the red-hot boiler should set the building on fire. One photograph was taken of the grisly scene and then officers, wearing heavy gloves, carefully lifted the disembodied legs out of the furnace and onto a blanket that had been spread on the floor. The coroner

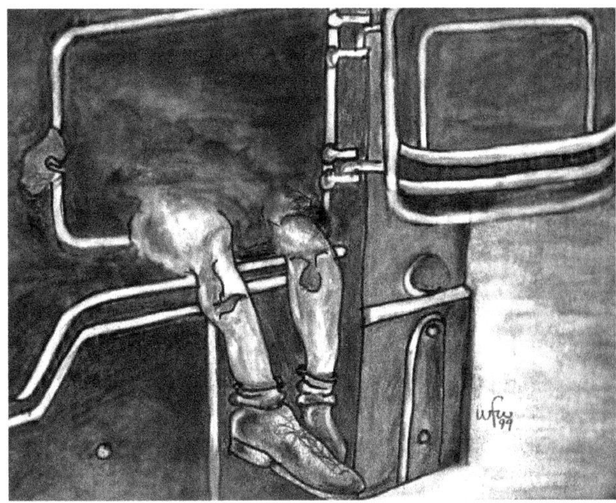

The remains of Ray Colbath as they were discovered by his brother-in-law. Sketch by the author made from the only photo taken at the scene of his death. *Author's collection.*

was called, and after examining the legs, he drew a blood sample from each one. The legs were then removed to the Sheboygan County morgue.

Since investigators had little to go on, the big question on everyone's mind was, what happened? Had the victim been murdered? Suicide was mentioned but considered unlikely. Was it even possible for a man to end his life by crawling into a roaring furnace? The badly shaken brother-in-law, who had regained some of his composure, identified the pile of clothing found on the floor as being that of Ray Colbath. The coroner developed the theory that if Ray had been alive when he entered the furnace there should be gases such as carbon dioxide and carbon monoxide in the blood stream, which would have been inhaled before the victim died. But this was before the time of forensic crime scene investigation. The problem now was who could test the blood samples to determine if the gases were present in the blood samples. Then someone thought of the chemistry teacher at the old Central High School—maybe he could help. The chemistry teacher was contacted, and after some hesitation, he stated that he thought he could run the required tests. The blood samples were turned over to him, and the testing procedure began. Several days later, the teacher contacted the coroner and stated that he had definitely found traces of the two gases in the victim's blood sample. This new evidence strongly indicated that Ray Colbath was alive when he entered the blazing furnace. Now the question was how did Ray end up in the furnace?

Investigators began to try to piece together the events of that gruesome night. Dozens of interviews were held, all to no avail. The only person who could shed any kind of light on Ray's last days was his sister. She related that a few days before his death he had gone to see the doctor, and when he returned home he seemed depressed. Had the doctor given him bad news? The more the police investigated, the less they understood the last hours of Ray Colbath. Many questions about his strange death remained. Could a man really jump into a roaring, red-hot furnace? If he did commit suicide, why did he take off his clothes? Was he murdered? If so, why didn't the murderer push the body all the way into the furnace? And again, the question of the clothes—why would a killer go through the trouble of taking his clothes off? What possible motive would anyone have to kill Ray? To this day, these and many other questions remain.

The coroner impaneled a coroner's jury, and all the evidence was presented to them. After a lengthy deliberation, they handed down the verdict as follows: "We the jury find that Ray Colbath died by his own hand." To this day, the death of Ray Colbath remains one of Sheboygan's most puzzling and enduring mysteries.

A Christmas Gift of Poison

Christmas is normally a time of celebration, joy, gift giving and goodwill to men. In the early part of the twentieth century, the season was a very social and festive time. It was a time to put on your Sunday best and visit all the relatives. Everywhere groups of people could be seen carrying piles of gaily wrapped gifts. It was a time of parties, dances and family reunions. But in the year 1910 for three Plymouth families, the gay holiday season turned into a nightmare of near death and terror. For them, instead of receiving holiday goodwill, they became victims of a weird attempted murder plot.

Just before Christmas 1910, on a cold, crisp winter evening, Mr. and Mrs. E.E. Eastman and their teenage daughter, Sarah, returned home from attending a high school event. As the Eastman family climbed the steps to their front porch, they were pleasantly surprised to find a package wrapped in colorful Christmas paper, addressed to Sarah, propped up against the front door. The mystery package gave no clue as to who it may have been from. Sarah's father good-naturedly teased her about a secret admirer. Blushing, she picked up the mysterious package and carried it into the house. Thinking that perhaps the mystery gift giver had included a note or a card inside, Sarah tore the wrappings off the book-shaped package. Eagerly lifting the cover of the beautiful box, she was delighted to find row

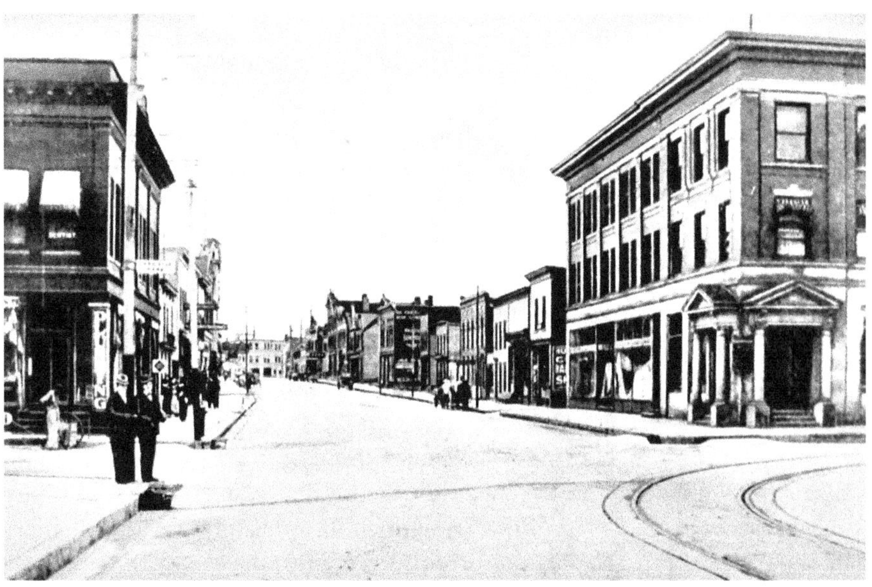

Plymouth, Wisconsin, at it appeared in 1910 when the strange poisoning case occurred. *Courtesy Sheboygan County Historic Research Center.*

upon row of what appeared to be very fine chocolate candies. In the year 1910, very seldom were chocolate candies ever found in the home except on very special occasions. Sarah selected a piece of the candy and slowly ate it, savoring the rich chocolate flavor. She then passed the box to her father, who also ate a piece of the rare treat. Sarah's mother declined to eat any of the candy, as she was not a great lover of chocolate. Sarah then replaced the cover and carefully put the box away.

Within less than an hour, both Mr. Eastman and his daughter became violently ill. Both of them suffered the same symptoms: severe abdominal cramping, muscle spasms and difficulty breathing. Realizing that both her husband and daughter were dangerously ill, Mrs. Eastman frantically placed a call to their family doctor, who, upon hearing the symptoms exhibited by the two Eastman's, rushed to their home. After a quick examination of his patients, the shocked doctor expressed to the stunned Mrs. Eastman the opinion that both father and daughter had ingested poison!

Throughout a long night, the doctor did his best to try to counteract the unknown poison. With the first light of a gray dawn, Sarah began to show improvement, but her father, if anything, seemed to be worse. The doctor expressed the fear that the elder Eastman might not survive the horrifying incident. Around noon of the day following the poisoning, it became evident that Mr. Eastman would survive.

Word of the strange illness that had struck the Eastmans spread through the small town like wildfire. Fear gripped Plymouth. Was it a contagious disease? Could it spread to the rest of town? After researching the symptoms, the doctor made a public statement that the Eastman's had been victims of strychnine poisoning. The doctor further stated that he thought the source of the poison was the chocolate candy they both had eaten. The stunned community came to the realization that someone in their community had fiendishly tried to murder members of the Eastman family.

As stunning as the news of the poisoning of the Eastman family was, it was only the beginning. Several days after the first incident, the Plymouth police chief announced to the incredulous city that two more families had received boxes of chocolates from an anonymous person, both of which he believed contained poison. This was beyond comprehension for the citizenry of Plymouth; things like this did just not happen in their neat, quiet, law-abiding town. It was now abundantly clear that some deranged person was loose in their midst. Everywhere you went, in barbershops, taverns, on the streets and in the stores that lined Mill Street, the poison candy was the sole topic of discussion. It is safe to say that not one single piece of chocolate candy was sold in Plymouth that Christmas season.

Plymouth authorities urged restraint, pointing out that possibly a terrible error had been made at the factory that manufactured the candy and that through some blunder strychnine had been accidentally induced into the candy when it was manufactured. However, when the candy was closely examined, it was found that someone had carefully sliced off the bottom of the chocolates, removed some of the contents and replaced it with the deadly poison. The bottoms of the chocolates were then reattached, leaving very little evidence that they had been tampered with. Even more frightening was the fact that some of the candies had more strychnine placed in them than others. The chemist stated that some of the candy had enough poison in them to kill a horse! The examining chemist stated that had the Eastmans eaten one of the chocolates that were heavily laced with the poison, they would surely have died; it was by pure chance that they had not. Plymouth Police Chief O'Connell was now clearly faced with three counts of attempted murder. Local newspapers ran a banner headline crying "A Dastardly Crime Has Been Committed."

The chief was baffled; a crime of this scope was beyond his experience. He needed help! He turned to the Sheboygan Police Department and the world-famous Pinkerton Detective Agency for assistance. Chief Scheck of Sheboygan and the Pinkerton detective both assured the beleaguered chief that a thorough investigation would be made and a quick arrest would follow. It would turn out that they were being just a mite overly optimistic.

As could be expected, the pressure on local authorities was intense; the good taxpaying citizens of Plymouth wanted results, and soon! They wanted answers. Who was the fiend who tried to kill members of three prominent families, and why?

About the only fact that was clear was that the perpetrator seemed to know Sarah, as the first package was addressed to her by name. Even more confusing was the fact that the three families involved had nothing in common, except that the heads of household were all well-to-do businessmen in the Plymouth area. The local media described the person responsible for the poisoning as one who was an "unknown deviate with a depraved mind."

Rumors began to fly that certain influential people in the community were trying to hinder the investigation, fearful that embarrassing information would come out. Charges and countercharges were angrily hurled back and forth. The three families involved got together and offered a reward of $500 leading to the arrest and conviction of the guilty party, a princely sum in those days.

On January 24, 1911, it was rumored that a confession had been obtained by authorities. The only comment the Plymouth police chief would make was that "progress is being made."

On January 31, 1911, it was reported that an arrest had been made in the poison case. The whole city of Plymouth was agog with excitement. The question on everybody's mind was who was the foul criminal? The announcement that the whole town was dying to hear was made by Sherriff Hoppe. The sheriff identified the suspect as Louis Brickner, age twenty-eight, of the Elkhart Lake area. In the unrestricted prose of the day, Brickner was described by the *Sheboygan Press* as "not too bright and girl crazy." What this had to do with the case was never explained. With the news that the foul fiend they all feared was behind bars, the city of Plymouth rejoiced. It was then learned that the man who cracked the case was none other than C.P. O'Brien of the Pinkerton Detective Agency. Authorities refused to reveal on just what evidence Brickner had been arrested.

Suddenly, the case took a new twist when it was reported that a young lady in Plymouth had received an obscene postcard that had been mailed from the Elkhart Lake area. What interested officers most about the postcard was that the handwriting on the card seemed to match the handwriting on the gift card that was attached to the package of poison candy the Eastman family had received. The services of a handwriting expert were clearly needed. A nationally recognized handwriting expert from Milwaukee was brought in to examine the questioned documents.

To muddy the waters even more, Otto Brickner, the brother of the suspect, came forward and claimed that his brother was innocent due to the fact that at the time the crime was being committed his brother was in Sheboygan at his home.

The city of Plymouth was in a great state of excitement over Brickner's arrest. The suspect was held in the county jail with a bail set at $2,500 and held for trial. Brickner could not post bail due to the family being "out of circumstances," as the media described it. District Attorney Collins assured everyone that Louis Brickner would pay for his heinous crime with a long jail sentence. The state further contended that the evidence they had was so compelling that he could not refute it. It seems that the main thrust of their prosecution was that the postcard the young lady received—as well as a weird letter whose contents were never disclosed that was delivered to the mayor of Plymouth—all were alleged to have been written by Brickner.

On the day of the preliminary hearing, the courtroom was jammed; Brickner was represented by Attorney Rooney of Plymouth. To everyone's great disappointment, the district attorney asked for a two-week postponement, as the highly regarded handwriting expert was not available. Brickner's attorney protested loudly, but the adjournment was granted.

The case was at last called before Judge Chaplin on February 23, 1911. District Attorney Collins stunned the standing-room-only courtroom when he asked for a dismissal of all charges against Brickner. Upon hearing the district attorney's request, the packed courtroom let out a collective gasp. It seems that the handwriting expert had come to the conclusion that Brickner had not written the gift card on the box of poison candy. The district attorney's request was granted, and Louis Brickner walked out of the courtroom absolved of all charges.

On March 16, the *Sheboygan Press* printed a small article stating that interest in the case of the poison candy had waned and no further action would be taken.

To this day, the long-forgotten case remains an unsolved mystery.

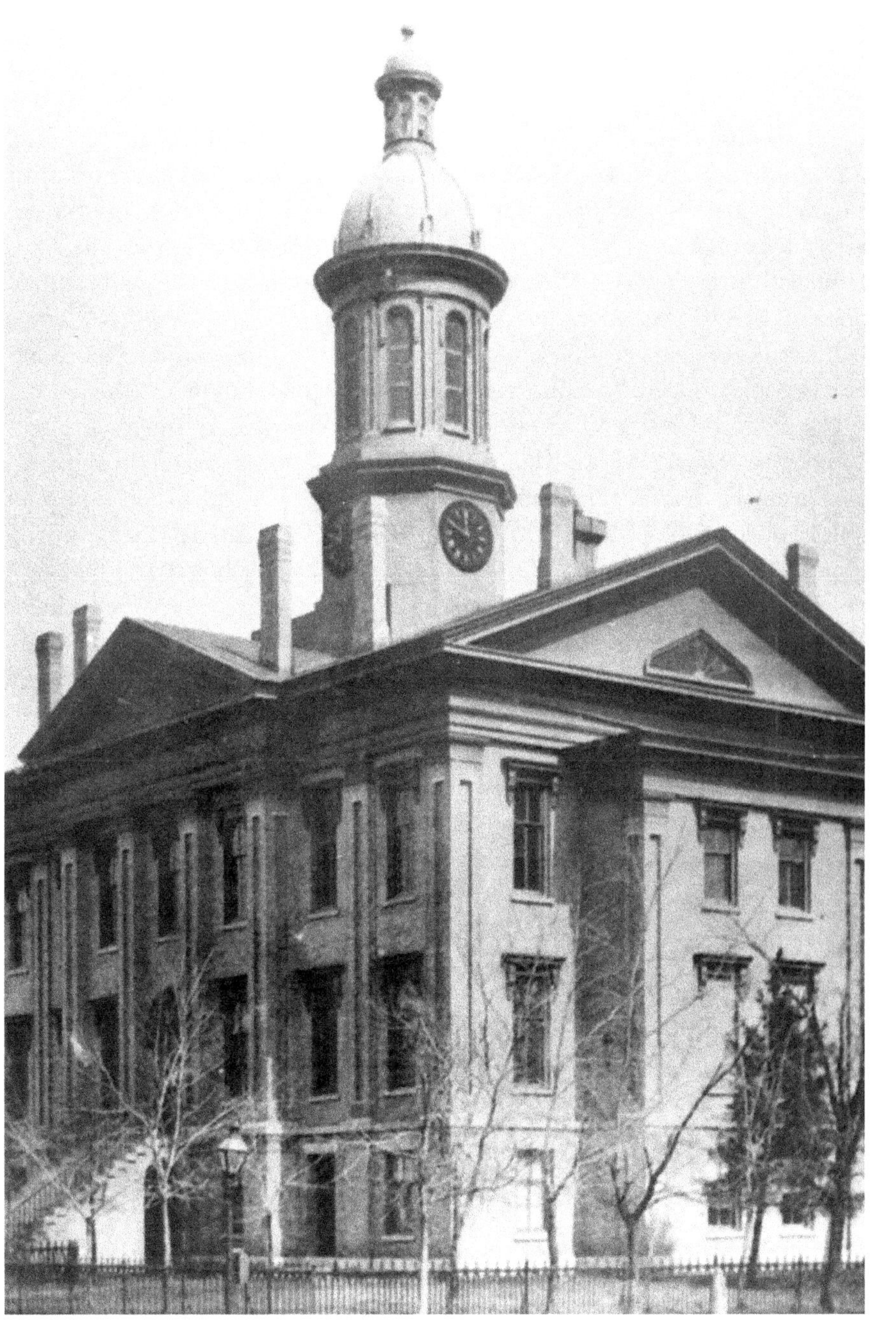

The old courthouse where the trial of Louis Brickner took place in 1911. *Author's collection.*

THE OPEN GATE

On the sunny early spring morning of April 19, 1852, little Frankie Bond, the two-and-a-half-year-old son of Dr. and Mrs. M.A. Bond, a prominent doctor in the city of Sheboygan Falls, played in his fenced-in front yard. Every ten minutes or so, Mrs. Bond would go to the window to check on Frankie. It was on one of these checks that, to her horror, she found the gate open and Frankie missing.

Later it was learned that a patient of Dr. Bonds had come to the Bond home to pick up medication that he ordered. Apparently when the patient left he did not close the front gate, and the little boy wandered away. A search was begun at once. With the help of neighbors, searchers asked nearly every person in the area if they had seen the little boy. It was learned from one that Frankie had been seen near Browns Hotel, then located at the corner of Pine and Broadway Avenue. Others claimed they saw a boy fitting Frankie's description talking to a strange man; this alleged sighting was never verified.

Thinking that Frankie may have fallen into the Sheboygan River that roars through Sheboygan Falls over several rapids and low waterfalls, searchers began to drag the river. The river was dragged from Sheboygan Falls to Lake Michigan, a distance of ten miles or more. No sign of the boy was found. The surrounding area was checked for miles in every direction, on foot and on horseback, but not a single clue to Frankie's whereabouts was ever discovered. Frankie Bond had vanished.

CHAPTER 4
TALES OF STRANGE HAPPENINGS

THE GREAT INDIAN SCARE

When the first settlers arrived in the area that was to become Sheboygan, they soon came to realize that the Indians living in dense forests around them seemed to accept them, and very little trouble occurred. But there was always an undercurrent of fear and doubt; after all, they were savages, were they not? How could you trust someone who was so different than you? Newspapers of the day often carried lurid tales of savages killing, raping and burning whole settlements to the ground. Over the years, many of the local Indians came to be known by the settlers and on occasion would come into town; on these occasions, their presence often caused a stir. Even though some of the Indians were well known by the settlers, they were never quite trusted.

The story of the "Great Indian Scare" has been told many times. It is a classic tale of mass hysteria and clearly demonstrates how prejudice, unrestrained fear and blind panic can affect tens of thousands of people based on nothing more than vague rumors. In those days of poor communication, the panic unbelievably spread quickly along the lakeshore, from Green Bay to Chicago, in a matter of days.

The year was 1862; the blood bath known as the Civil War roared on, seemingly endlessly. The war news was not good; it seemed that on every occasion when Southern and Northern troops met in combat, the South always won. People were getting nervous; what if the South won? Would they invade and occupy the Northern territories? Then there were the

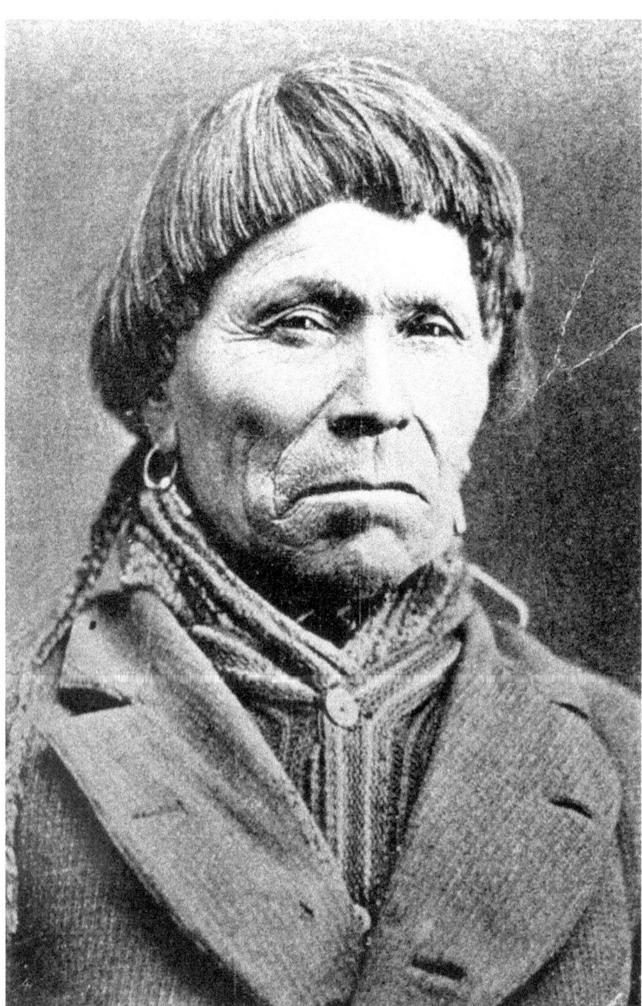

Old Solomon, the best-known and most trusted Indian who lived in the Sheboygan area. *Courtesy Sheboygan County Historic Research Center.*

Indians to worry about. After all, Sheboygan and the surrounding territories were still considered wilderness by most people in the East. There was no telling how many Indians could be lurking in the dense forests that still surrounded the small city of Sheboygan. September 3, 1862, was perhaps one of the most amazing days in the history of our city; it is the day of the Great Indian Scare.

It was a warm, early autumn day with a clear blue sky; the leaves in the forests around the city were just beginning to change colors. Out in the countryside, farmers were well along with the fall harvest that was proving to be a bountiful one. In Sheboygan, on this idyllic day, several men were seated on a bench in front of the Kossuth House, a popular Sheboygan hotel that was located at the present-day intersection of North Eighth and Center Avenue. They were discussing at great length the war news and local gossip. It was mid-afternoon, and only a very few people were on the streets. All in all, the entire general atmosphere was quiet and sleepy; that would very soon change.

Suddenly, the loafers in front of the hotel were startled to hear the rapid pounding of hooves coming down Eighth Street from the north. Looking toward the sound, the men saw a cloud of dust and a horse and rider traveling at breakneck speed. The rider was shouting something unintelligible as he lashed his mount to run even faster. Seeing the three men in front of the hotel, the rider reined his lathered horse to a sudden stop. The unknown rider, his face contorted with fear, leapt from his horse even before it had come to a full stop. As the frantic man hit the ground, he stumbled and fell, but quickly regained his footing.

He ran toward the men shouting, "Injuns are coming, Injuns are coming!" The men jumped to their feet, casting bewildered looks at one another. Injuns? Where? "They're comin' down from Green Bay, thousands of 'em, killin', robbin', raping all the women and tearin' babies from their mother arms and throwin 'em into burning buildings they set afire. Green Bay, Algoma, Kewanee, Manitowoc are all burned to the ground. When they come to a farm they're burnin' all the barns, settin' crops afire and stealing everything they can lay hands on, everything in their path is gone. You better make a stand or get out; if I was you folks I would get out!"

The unknown messenger then remounted his exhausted steed and sped away in a cloud of dust. Having heard the commotion, people had begun to gather and listen in stunned silence to the distraught messenger's every word. The news of the bloodthirsty horde sweeping down on them spread throughout the city like wildfire. People began running out of downtown buildings and rushing home to see to the protection of their families. Within less than an hour, every hardware store in the city had sold every last gun it had in stock. They soon ran out of gunpowder and shot. Before long, not an ounce of gunpowder could be had in the city. Then the people began to buy butcher knives, which they tied to long poles to form makeshift spears. In sheer panic they frantically bought anything that had a sharp edge and could be used as a weapon. Axes, hatchets and pitchforks were all quickly sold out.

City leaders dispatched riders to Sheboygan Falls, Plymouth and area farms with the grim news that a horde of blood-crazed savages was on the way. Guns that had not fired a shot since the Revolutionary War were taken out of attics and loaded. In Plymouth, an elderly man appeared on the street in a Prussian army uniform, complete with a spiked helmet and a rusty sword, from the days when he had served in that army. A terrified young farm wife whose husband was away, on hearing the news, ran from her home to Plymouth, over two miles away, carrying the only thing she thought to save: a still warm pumpkin pie.

Captain Marchner, leader of the city militia, marshaled his men under arms, swearing he would defend Sheboygan to the last man. Before long, wagons piled high with personal belongings and frightened farm families began to pour into Sheboygan, choking every road leading into town. Apparently the multitude of refugees felt there was safety in numbers. In no time at all, almost every street and alley in the city was clogged with wagons and frightened people. One wagon that rushed into the city was loaded with a pile of personal possessions; and there on the very top, in a rocking chair fastened securely to the wagon, sat an elderly lady hanging on for dear life.

Some people harnessed up the family horse, hitched up the wagon, threw into it what they could quickly grab and rode out of town as fast as they

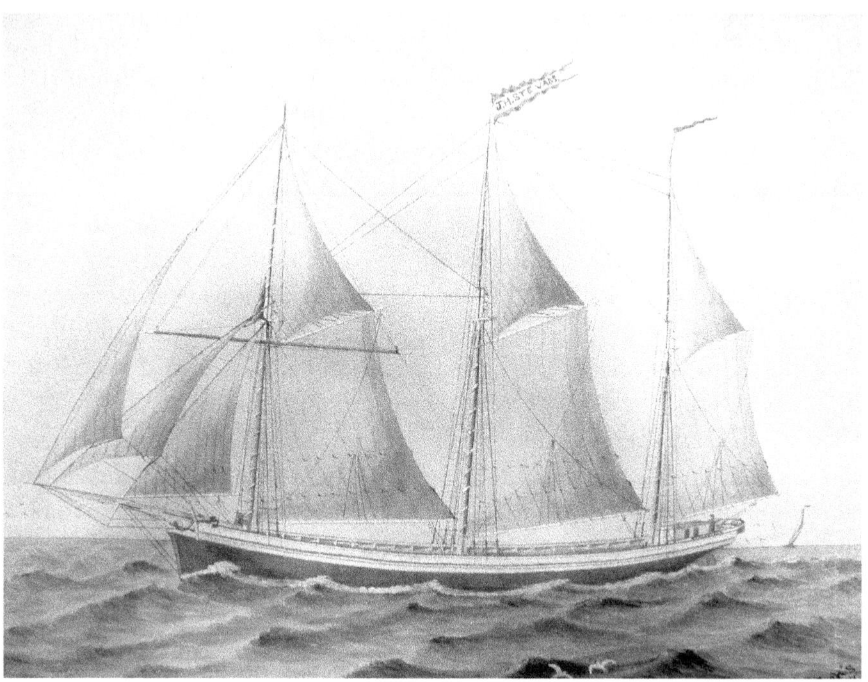

The schooner *J.H. Stevens* is typical of the many ships that were tied up in the harbor during the Great Indian Scare. *Author's collection.*

could. Other people rushed to the harbor, where a dozen or so ships were unloading or taking on cargo. Once at the harbor, frantic people offered ship captains ridiculous sums of money to take them on board and set sail at once. Some of the captains did take passengers on board and set sail; others refused.

In the county, terrified farmers turned their livestock loose in hopes that the savages would find not them. Farm wives gathered what family valuables they had and buried them out in their fields. Farmers then herded their families out into the cornfields to hide from what they felt would be certain death if the Indians caught them. Some even vowed to kill their own families and then themselves before they would allow their loved ones to be slaughtered…or worse. Then came the darkness, which they feared almost as much as the unseen oncoming horde.

As darkness fell, every sound became an Indian creeping through the cornfield; every shadow was an object to be feared. Throughout the long, terrifying night, families cowered in fear, clinging to one another in their fields.

Captain Marchner assembled the militia and ordered them to march to the north city limits. The assembled grim-faced men marched out the Calumet Road, today's Calumet Drive, and set up a roadblock. Apparently the militia felt that the marauding Indians were going to form into a marching unit and march down the Calumet Road. Tension in the city was so thick you could cut it with a knife. On the barricade in Sheboygan, the militia gripped their weapons tightly, their nerves strung tighter than bowstrings. Then they heard movement in the brush—the Indians were creeping up on them! Someone fired, and then they all fired into the dark. The militiamen heard a groan and then a thud of a body hitting the ground. One of the militiamen remarked, "That's one injun that ain't going to scalp no one." All at once, they saw the flickering and dancing of flames in the sky. Here was proof they were under attack; the Indians were burning out some hapless farmer.

The long, terrifying night slowly ground on without further incident. The imminent attack they all feared never came. As the first light of dawn streaked the dark skies, it was decided to send out a patrol to try and determine just where the attacking forces were. Volunteers were called for; several of the weary defenders came forward and formed a patrol. Cautiously, the patrol stepped out from behind the barricade. First they searched the brush to try to find out who or what they had shot the night before. As they searched the brush they found the answer: the bullet-riddled carcass of a Holstein cow. Sheepishly, they started out down the road to check on the fire they had all seen the night before. As the patrol came around a bend in the road, they all stopped. There was the evidence they all sought: the ruins of a burnt-out barn. Standing amidst the mass of burnt timbers stood a dejected farmer and his wife, their hands and face streaked in soot. The patrol approached him and asked, "How many injuns were there?" The puzzled farmer asked, "Injuns? There weren't no Injuns" The patrol leader asked, "Didn't they set fire to your barn?" The perplexed man replied, "Heck no, I tipped over a lantern and set fire to the hay. Then I ran outside and rang the fire bell like crazy and no one came. Where the hell was everybody?" The patrol leader tried to explain to the incredulous man just what had been taking place. The baffled famer said in amazement, "You believed a wild tale like that?" The patrol members cast embarrassed looks back and forth. The farmer just shook his head and trudged back to the ruins of his barn to try to save what he could. The exhausted man by now was sure he had just talked to a band of lunatics.

The heavily armed patrol moved on down the road, where they soon encountered a rider who told them he had just come from Manitowoc. They anxiously inquired of him how many Indians he had seen. The rider, totally puzzled at being interrogated by the armed group of men, scratched his head and said, "I saw a couple of them about two weeks ago." The patrolmen stared at one another. "Was Manitowoc destroyed?" they asked. "Not when I last saw it late yesterday," the rider replied. The horseman nervously clutched his rifle, unsure of what was going on. Again, the patrolmen explained to the stranger their purpose for being heavily armed and asking what seemed like ridiculous questions. The rider spurred his horse forward and furtively looked back over his shoulder as he left the now chagrined group standing in the middle of the dusty road.

It soon became apparent that there weren't ten thousand Indians or one thousand, or one hundred or even ten Indians attacking—there were none! As quickly as they could, the patrol marched back to the barricade and explained what they had found, or more correctly, what they had not found. As the militia marched back to the center of town, they were bombarded by a thousand questions from anxious residents. Soon the word spread. It had all been a hoax! One by one, the wagons turned and headed back home, everyone feeling just a bit foolish.

How the rumor was started was never learned. Unbelievably, in an era when a letter could take weeks to travel a few hundred miles, the panic spread from Green Bay to Chicago in a matter of days.

To this day, the Great Indian Scare of 1862 remains one of the most bizarre events in the history of Sheboygan. Many questions remain. Why had literally tens of thousands of people from an area covering the entire western shore of Lake Michigan been so willing to accept at face value an entirely unsubstantiated rumor? Not one person who reported the alleged Indian attack had actually witnessed the "facts" they were reporting. No one seemed to question if the so-called Indian raid was really taking place; everyone just accepted the reports and reacted in blind panic. The entire episode was a classic example of mass hysteria. Perhaps the fact that a widely reported horrific Indian raid had taken place one month earlier on August 19 at New Ulm, Minnesota, with great loss of life had an effect on their judgment. The real reasons for the Great Indian Scare of 1862 are forever lost in the mists of time.

The Ship Without a Captain

In more recent times, the mystery that took place on board the steamer *McFarland* just off our shores defies explanation. In fact, the mystery took place in an area that many people feel possesses the same mysterious powers inherent in the infamous Bermuda Triangle. The so-called triangle on Lake Michigan has been said to cover an area that begins at Ludington, Michigan, south to Benton Harbor, Michigan, northwest across Lake Michigan to Manitowoc, Wisconsin, and then east, back across the lake to Ludington. In this triangular area, it is recorded that strange and unexplained disappearances have taken place. People, ships and aircraft have all disappeared without a trace and with no explanation. Not only have there been inexplicable disappearances in this area, but there have also been numerous reports from reliable sources who have claimed to have seen what can only be described as "sea monsters."

On April 28, 1937, one of the strangest mysteries of the Great Lakes took place just off the shores of Sheboygan, and well within the so-called Lake Michigan Triangle. It was early in the shipping season, and a great deal of ice still clogged the northern reaches of the Great Lakes. The *O.M. McFarland* was commanded by fifty-eight-year-old George R. Doner, who had spent most of his adult life sailing the Great Lakes. The *McFarland* had taken on board a cargo of 9,800 tons of coal at Erie, Pennsylvania, and then headed through the Great Lakes bound for Port Washington, Wisconsin. As the *McFarland* passed through the passage at the top of the Great Lakes, it encountered a great deal of ice. This and the fact that the *McFarland* was having trouble with both its fore and aft compasses kept Captain Doner on the bridge of his ship for almost thirty-six hours without sleep. Once into the warmer and ice-free waters of Lake Michigan, the exhausted captain told the first mate to take command, as he was leaving the bridge to get some rest. Captain Doner also ordered that he was to be awakened when the ship passed Sheboygan so that he could bring it into its destination at Port Washington. According to crew members, they said the captain was in reasonable sprits, as it was his birthday. After Captain Doner left the bridge, the ship continued south toward Port Washington without incident. As the ship passed Sheboygan, the first mate sent a steward to the captain's cabin to awaken him. However, a short time later the steward returned, saying he could get no response from the captain. Puzzled, the first mate sent the second mate to try to waken the captain. After repeatedly knocking on the door and receiving no response, the officer opened the door and, to his surprise, found the room empty!

Thinking that perhaps Doner had gone for a cup of coffee and a bite to eat, he checked the galley, but the captain was not there either. Then he checked the head and the shower area…nothing. Slowly, the realization that Captain Doner was missing became clear to him.

The second mate rushed back to the bridge. The first mate immediately asked him when the captain would be reassuming command, as they were getting closer to Port Washington by the minute. Breathlessly, the second mate related that he could not find Captain Doner. The astonished first mate inquired loudly, "What do you mean you can't find him?" The second mate replied, "So help me I checked his cabin and it was empty, then I checked the ship from stem to stern, but I couldn't find him. None of the crew has seen him either; he's just gone!"

The incredulous first mate ordered the second mate to take over the bridge while he conducted his own search, and he rushed below. Crew members were organized into a search party, and every nook and cranny of the big ship was searched, but to no avail. Captain Doner had disappeared!

By now, the *McFarland* was approaching Port Washington harbor with the first mate in command. The ship was brought into port and tied up at the coal docks. The incident was reported to the Coast Guard and the local sheriff for further investigation. Once again the ship was searched, and not a clue to the captain's whereabouts was found.

The Coast Guard put out a message to all ships in the area, informing them of Captain Doner's disappearance and to watch for his body, possibly floating in the lake.

The remains of the twenty-five-year veteran of sailing the Great Lakes were never recovered, and the mystery of Captain Doner's disappearance from his ship, in good weather, has never been solved.

Proponents of the Lake Michigan Triangle theory are not perplexed at all over the disappearance of Captain Donner. After all, the *O.M. McFarland* was sailing through the very heart of the mysterious Lake Michigan Triangle!

Flight 2501 Is Missing

The weather report for June 24, 1950, called for warm, humid conditions, with temperatures reaching ninety degrees and the possibility of a few local thunderstorms. There was not a hint of the impending disaster the weather would, before long, inflict.

In Sheboygan, June 24 had been set aside to celebrate the installation of the state-of-the-art mercury vapor lights that had been installed along North Eighth Street. A parade was planned, along with speeches by local dignitaries and a band concert, to wind up the festivities.

As the weather report predicted, Friday, June 24 dawned hot and humid. The new lighting was scheduled to be turned on for the first time at 9:00 p.m. CST. By 6:00 p.m., crowds were already gathering along North Eighth Street to be able to get a good view of the parade.

At the same time at LaGuardia field in New York City, Northwest Airlines Captain Robert Lind, his co-pilot, Vern Wolf, and their stewardess, Bonnie Ann Feldman, were busily preparing their big DC-4, four-engine airliner for a nonstop flight to Minneapolis, Minnesota. Northwest flight 2501, besides its crew of three, would be carrying fifty-five passengers that day. The co-pilot, Wolf, had carefully checked the weather report along their flight path and noted that there was a possibility of scattered thunderstorms over Wisconsin but nothing to cause great concern. Wolf informed the pilot, who advised Wolf to keep a close watch on the weather reports and to keep him informed.

By 7:00 p.m. EST, passengers began to board flight 2501 for the long, nonstop flight to Minneapolis. At about 7:15 p.m., Captain Lind began to turn over the big Pratt and Whitney R2000 1450-horsepower engines until all four of them were running smoothly. The DC-4 was by no means a small aircraft. With a wingspan of 117 feet, 6 inches and a length of almost 94 feet, it was a giant of the skies for its day.

Captain Lind contacted the tower and was given clearance to taxi to the end of the runway. The silver giant reached the end of the runway and turned into the wind to await clearance for takeoff. At 7:25 p.m. EST, flight 2501 was given permission to take off. Pilot Lind advanced the four throttles, and the big engines roared to full power. Four huge propeller blades clawed at the air as the airliner gained speed, and as its wings generated lift, it gently and gracefully lifted off the runway, tucked its landing gear into its belly and soared into the darkening early night sky, carrying fifty-eight souls to their destiny. As flight 2501 disappeared from sight, the last rays of the setting sun turned its polished aluminum skin to gold.

Back in Sheboygan, the parade had just begun when, suddenly, ominous blue black clouds blotted out the setting sun. Like some onrushing evil monster, the mass of boiling clouds covered the sky. Then the winds struck, howling like a demented banshee. The wind roared through town, uprooting trees, stripping shingles from roofs and tearing down utility wires. In Sheboygan County, near Batavia, a huge tree was uprooted and flung across a moving car. The driver was killed instantly, but his wife and son seated next to him were uninjured.

Sheboygan was a total shambles; Camp Haven, a military camp that was located near the village of Haven near today's present Whistling Straights golf course, suffered severe damage and could not function for two weeks.

Onboard the westbound airliner, the passengers and crew were unaware of the oncoming gale. At 11:15 p.m. EST, Captain Lind reported that flight 2501 was passing over Battle Creek, Michigan, and was flying level at 3,500 feet. Normally the aircraft would have crossed the lake near Chicago, but due to weather in the area Captain Lind asked for permission to change his course farther to the north to avoid bad weather in his path. Northwest control in Chicago granted him permission to divert farther north so that flight 2501, upon crossing the lake, would pass over Milwaukee. In a few moments, Captain Lind again called Chicago control with the estimate that he would pass over Milwaukee in about twenty minutes at 1:37 p.m. EST.

At 1:13 a.m. EST, flight 2501 was approaching the eastern shore of Lake Michigan, at which time Captain Lind again called Chicago control and asked permission to descend to 2,500 feet due to bad weather in the area. This time permission was denied, as there was other traffic at that altitude. This communication was the last ever heard from flight 2501.

When the airliner vanished with the fifty-eight persons on board, it carried 2,500 gallons of fuel, 80 gallons of oil and 490 pounds of mail and cargo.

When the DC-4, which was scheduled to pass over Milwaukee at 1:37 p.m. EST, failed to arrive airline officials became anxious. They called flight 2501 repeatedly but received no answer. A call then went out to all control centers in the Midwest to try to contact the overdue plane; none succeeded. Northwest control then called all available air sea rescue units to stand by.

At 5:30 a.m. CST, Northwest Airline announced that it was quite clear that flight 2501, its passengers and crew were lost over Lake Michigan.

A massive search was immediately launched. Every available Coast Guard plane took to the air, and every Coast Guard vessel joined the search. Air force and Civil Air Patrol scoured the surface of the big lake for survivors. None was ever found. About twelve miles northwest of Benton Harbor, Michigan, a small debris field was located. Only a few of the items that were recovered were positively identified as having come from the missing aircraft. It was indicated, by the small size of the pieces of debris, that the DC-4 had hit the water with tremendous force, totally obliterating the aircraft. Several well-equipped teams of divers have tried to locate the wreckage of Northwest 2501, but none has succeeded.

Was the cause of the crash pilot error? Very unlikely, as both pilots had thousands of hours of safe flying. Was it structural failure, or bad weather? The true cause will never be known. The secret of what happened lies on the bottom of Lake Michigan beneath hundreds of feet of cold dark water, and the lake does not easily give up its secrets.

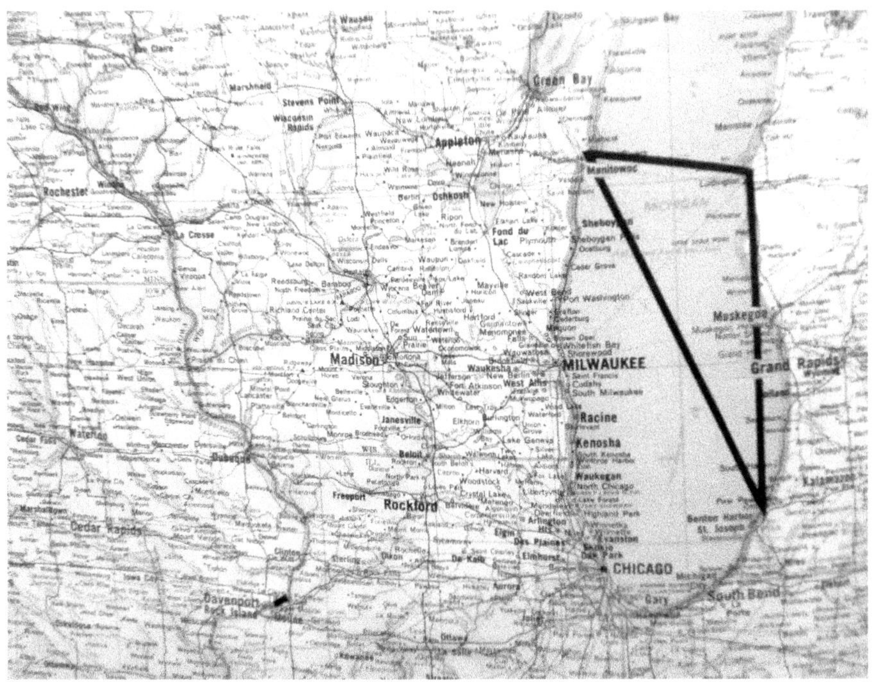

The alleged Lake Michigan Triangle. *Chart created by author.*

Believers in the Lake Michigan Triangle theory are convinced that the reason flight 2501 disappeared is simple. After all, the airliner was flying through the heart of the triangle, and it is just another victim that can be added to the long list of ships and planes that have vanished in this mysterious area.

CHAPTER 5

TRUE BITS OF LOCAL HISTORY

Some of Them Funny, Some of Them Sad, but All of Them True

In the year 1836, the population of Sheboygan was thirty-six persons.

For many years, Sheboygan was known simply as the "Mouth" because it was built on the mouth of the Sheboygan River.

During the great financial panic of late 1837, all but two people left the city. As they left, some people took their houses with them. The houses were loaded on barges and towed to Milwaukee. Indians moved into the abandoned homes and painted colorful native designs on the walls.

In 1837, the first mail service to Sheboygan was supplied by a letter carrier whose route was a rather long one. The route started in Chicago and ended in Green Bay, a distance of over two hundred miles, which he walked!

During the period of 1840 to about 1860, at least six railroads were proposed, but none was ever built.

Winter furs, which were thicker, were purchased from local trappers by fur traders and were of two kinds. Fine furs were obtained from beaver, otter, mink, fox, raccoon and skunk. Coarse furs, such as bear, deer and elk, were used for coats and lap robes.

In the early 1830s, a Mrs. Glass and her husband ran a small store at the mouth of the Sheboygan River. She sold coffee, sugar and sewing items such as pins, needles and thread. Whiskey was sold by the drink or by the quart. She also had several books that she would lend out, if she knew you. So it might be said that in the city of Sheboygan Mrs. Glass ran the first retail

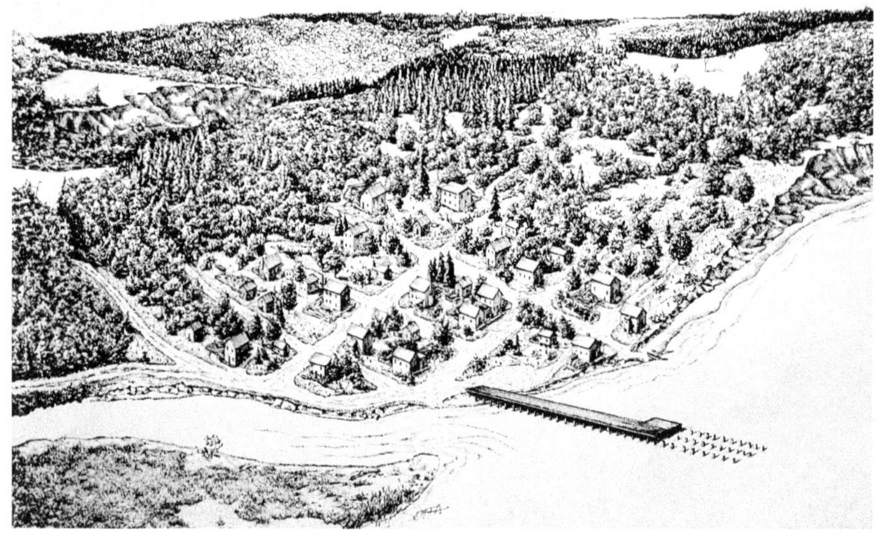

An artist's conception of what Sheboygan looked like in 1936. *Author's collection; artwork by Ed Sofa.*

establishment, the first tavern and the first lending library. It was also noted that she had to keep the whiskey under lock and key, as her husband on frequent occasions sampled the stock—to excess.

In the 1840s, early hotels, during busy times, made it a common practice to rent out the room to two, three or even four persons (of the same sex), all of whom had to sleep in one bed! Hotel patrons often complained that their bed partners failed to remove their shoes.

William Farnsworth, founder of Sheboygan, was so respected by local Indians that they gave him the name Ni-Kick, meaning the one who must be obeyed.

In 1846, the entire police department consisted of one man known as the town crier. It was his duty to make one round trip around the village each hour and then call out the time, such as, "Two o'clock and all is well."

A petition drawn up in 1847 was presented by H. Lyman and others praying the village board of trustees to take some measures to preserve the peace of the village from being disturbed night and day by Indians.

Also in the year 1847, the first printing press was brought to Sheboygan by George W. Gillette, who was editor and founder of Sheboygan's first newspaper, the *Sheboygan Mercury*. Gillette was the father of King Gillette, who invented the famous Gillette Safety Razor and founded a company that to

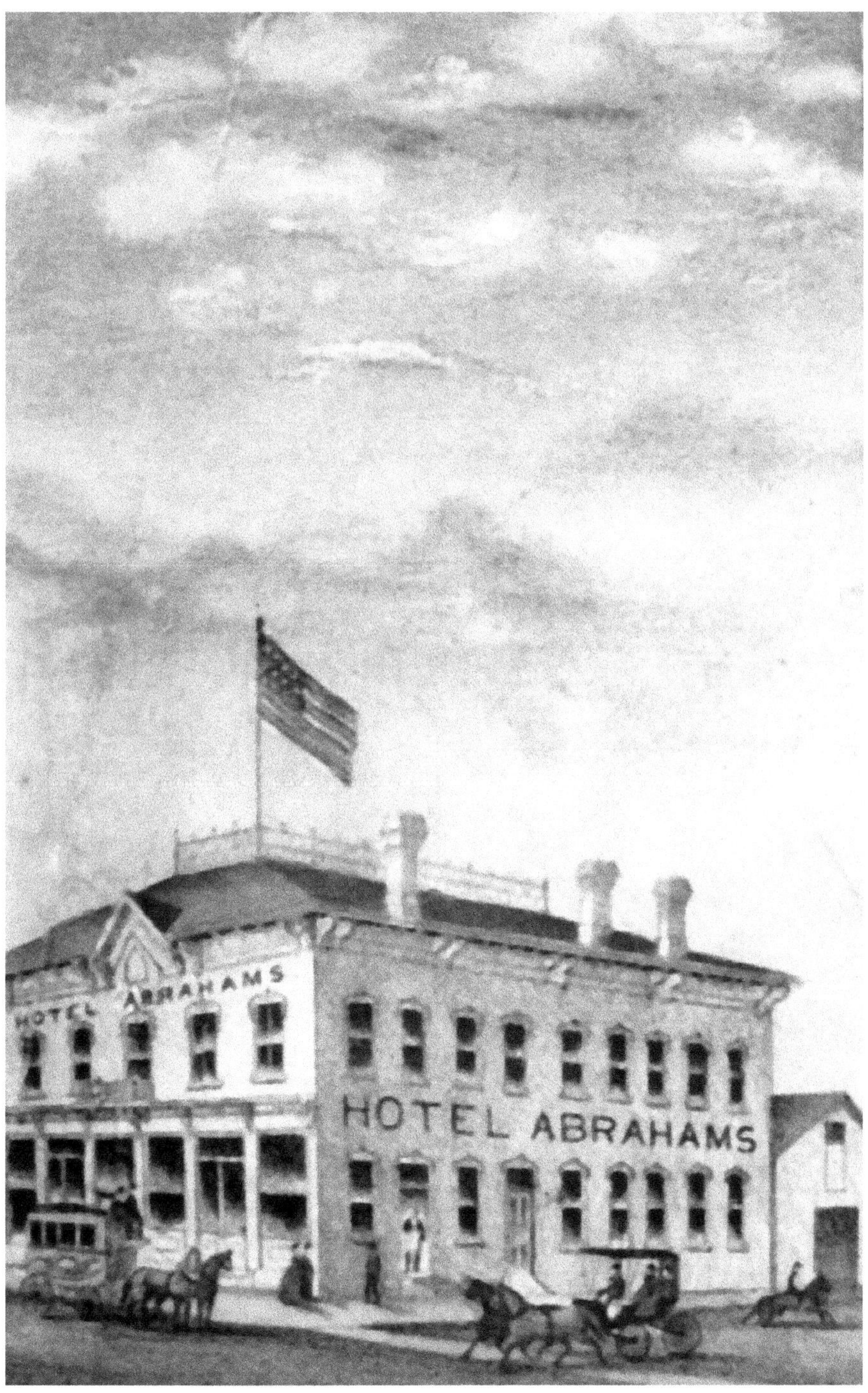

The Abraham's Hotel at North Eighth and Ontario Avenue, the first of four hotels built at this location. *Author's collection.*

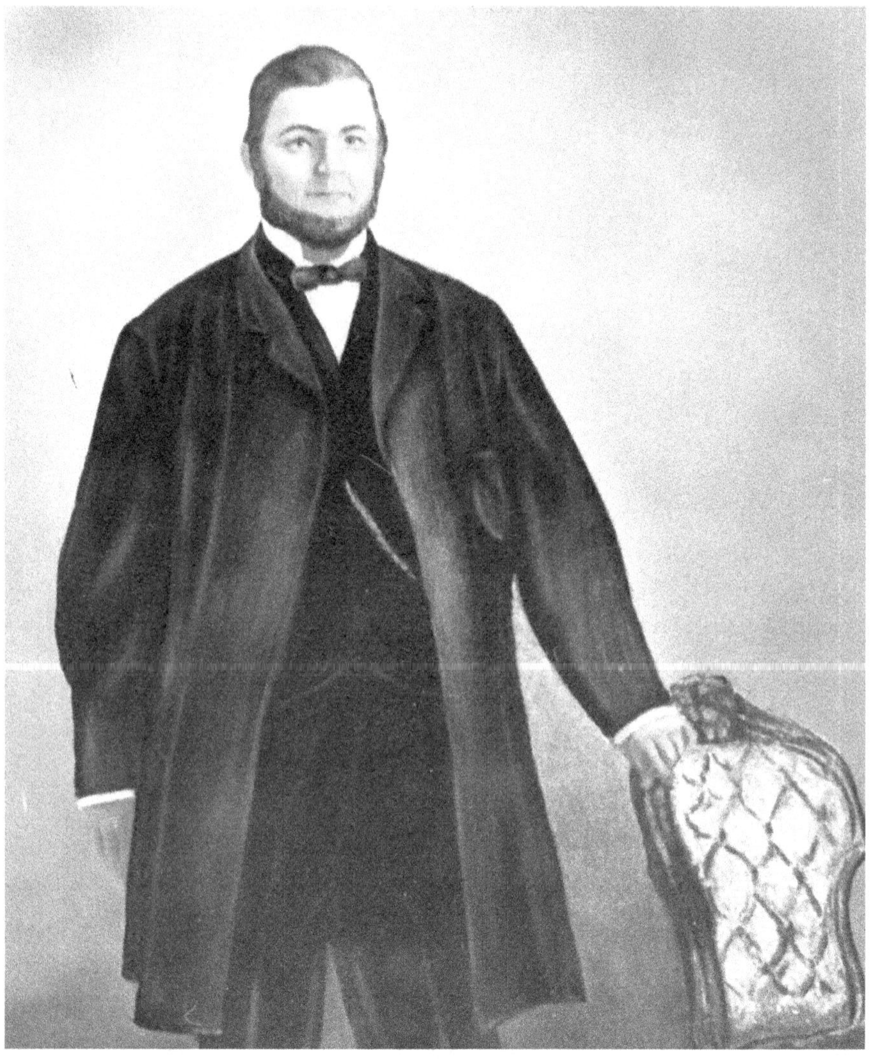

William Farnsworth, founder of Sheboygan. *Courtesy Sheboygan County Historic Research Center.*

this day carries his name. Since the *Mercury*'s publication, more than twenty-nine newspapers have come and gone in the city and county. One suspended publication after a mere five weeks. At least six of these newspapers were published in German.

The year 1847 was also recorded to have been one of the coldest on record. Sheboygan County experienced frost in every month of that year.

With all his land dealings and other business ventures, there is no record of William Farnsworth, founder of Sheboygan, ever owning property in the city of Sheboygan.

In 1848, Mr. Wade, owner of Wade House Stagecoach Inn, was appointed one of the commissioners to lay out the territorial road from Sheboygan to Fond du Lac. It's no surprise that the new road ran directly past Mr. Wade's property.

A bill of fifty cents was presented to the common council and allowed for removing a dead hog from the street.

The city employed a clock winder, whose job it was to set, maintain and wind all city clocks. He was paid more than a city firefighter.

Two petitions were submitted to the 1851 common council: one for and one against an ordinance prohibiting swine from running at large in the city. After failing to come to a consensus, the petitions were tabled.

In the early days of Sheboygan, the city had no city jail, and whenever a wrongdoer was given a jail sentence, he was confined in any building that could be securely locked. One person was found guilty of disorderly conduct, and the judge fined him two dollars, but the guilty party stated he had no money. The judge then said in lieu of the fine he would accept a jug of whiskey or the defendant could spend thirty days in jail—it was his choice. The defendant replied that he had a jug of whiskey but in no way was he going to give it to the judge. The guilty party was then hauled off and locked up in a horse barn, where for three days he banged on the walls and kicked on the door, demanding to be let out. He was not. Finally, after several more days, the prisoner agreed to turn over his jug of whiskey to the judge. He then left the improvised jail, a free man. What happened to the whiskey was not recorded.

In the 1850s in the Plymouth area, flour sold for five cents for two pounds, coffee was twelve cents a pound and tea was seventy-five cents a pound. Whiskey was sold at ten cents a quart, and butter was eleven cents a pound. A pair of shoes cost the princely sum of one dollar. A farm family's yearly grocery bill averaged about twenty-five dollars.

Deputy custom collector Michael Lynch reported that in 1854, 20,914 immigrants landed at Sheboygan. Residents complained that the city was beginning to assume the appearance of a gold mining camp with all its noise and clatter.

Drinking tanks for horses were placed at various points around the city. During hot weather, six horses and water wagons were used to keep the tanks full. The horses that drew firefighting equipment were not allowed to water at the city water tanks, as the fire department had its own tanks.

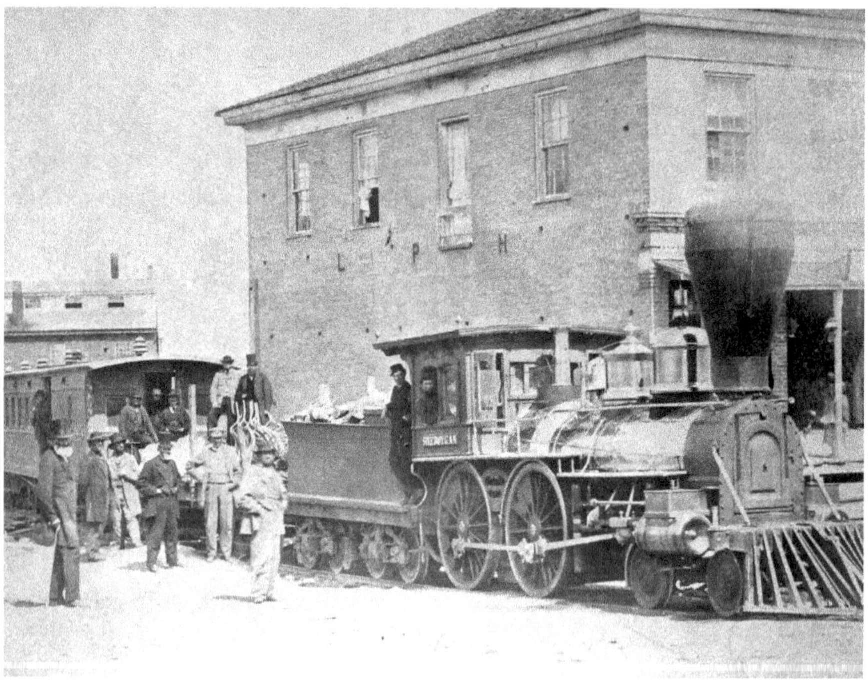

The first railroad train to run west out of Sheboygan, appropriately named the Sheboygan. *Courtesy Sheboygan County Historic Research Center.*

In fact, one firefighter was disciplined when he watered fire horses at a city water tank. While watering the horses, he was approached and berated by his superior, which led to an altercation during which the firefighter punched the superior officer in the nose!

In 1859, rail fare from Sheboygan to Sheboygan Falls was twenty cents, but if your trip was going to take you all the way to Plymouth that would cost you the handsome amount of sixty cents.

The census of 1860 showed that the majority of the city's population consisted of German-born immigrants. Most spoke only German.

Prior to a city waterworks, it was common practice for people who lived near Lake Michigan or the Sheboygan River to lay a pipe into the lake or river and pump water directly into their homes. It must be noted, however, that the river and the lake were a lot cleaner in those days.

The Liberty School of joint school district 11, which served the towns of Holland and Sherman, was built in 1868 at a cost of $160 and served the district for ninety-three years.

When a ship disappeared on the Great Lakes without a trace, which many did, sailors said the ship had sailed through a hole in the lake.

In 1872, it was recorded that 50 percent of students in the school system spoke German. The frustrated county superintendent of schools stated, "German students are making little attempt to learn English," even though school regulations of the time required them to do so.

In 1874, an item before the common council stated that neighbors in the area of Sixth Street to Seventh Street and Erie to Superior Avenue were complaining that owners of cows were allowing them to run at large in their neighborhood. The residents further complained that the cows were eating their gardens.

On days when the lake is very rough, the horizon over the lake looks very jagged, almost like a pine forest against the sky when seen from a distance. Sailors called this kind of horizon "Christmas trees."

The well in Fountain Park, drilled in 1875, was a fire well providing water to the fire department. This well is 1,475 feet deep and is an artesian well. A series of cisterns was dug on each corner south of Fountain Park along Eighth Street. The cisterns were approximately 16 feet deep and 8 feet in diameter. The first cistern located at Eighth and Ontario was connected directly to the well. Once that cistern was full, it overflowed into a pipe that ran to the next cistern, and so on down the entire length of Eighth Street until the last cistern was full and overflowed into the river. But, due to the heavy mineral content in the water, it could not be used, as it caused severe corrosion in the firefighting equipment, and the cisterns had to all be filled in again.

Finding the water unusable for firefighting, it was piped to a fountain, from which the park got its name. People were soon coming to the park to sample the water, which had a heavy metallic or mineral taste to it. Apparently, people felt that anything that tasted that bad had to be good for you, and they began to take the water home by the jug. Eventually, the water was bottled and shipped around the world. In fact, several cases were sent to the White House.

Records from 1876 indicate that at one time mental patients were kept in the county jail. A Mr. Jewet then erected a home for the mentally ill and was paid by the county $2.75 for each patient he cared for. The home was located just south of Plymouth in the village of Winooski, which has since disappeared.

In an 1878 school census, the number of children attending school in Sheboygan was found to be 1,459. Of that number, 38 students were enrolled in high school, 13 boys and 25 girls.

The average wage for a ten-hour day in a furniture factory in 1881 was ninety cents a day. The wages for a city worker during that same period were as low as twenty-five cents a day. At times, the city was unable to meet the payroll and gave city workers food coupons redeemable at a local grocery store that was owned by the city treasurer.

As strange as it may seem, Sheboygan, prior to 1881, had no system for house numbering or, for that matter, any street signs. In August 1881, a measure was passed creating a building numbering system and ordering street signs to be placed at all intersections.

Many of the area's worst snowstorms occurred not during the dead of winter but in March, such as the great snowstorm of 1881. For weeks, snow drifts as high as second-floor windows blocked Eighth Street.

Today, one of the often discussed topics in the school system is class size. In the year 1885, the Sheboygan school system enrolled 1,450 students while employing 20 teachers. That figures out to an average of 72.5 students per class!

Over the past 125 years or so, there were five ships named *Sheboygan*. The first was a sailing schooner, the second a side wheel steamer, the third a

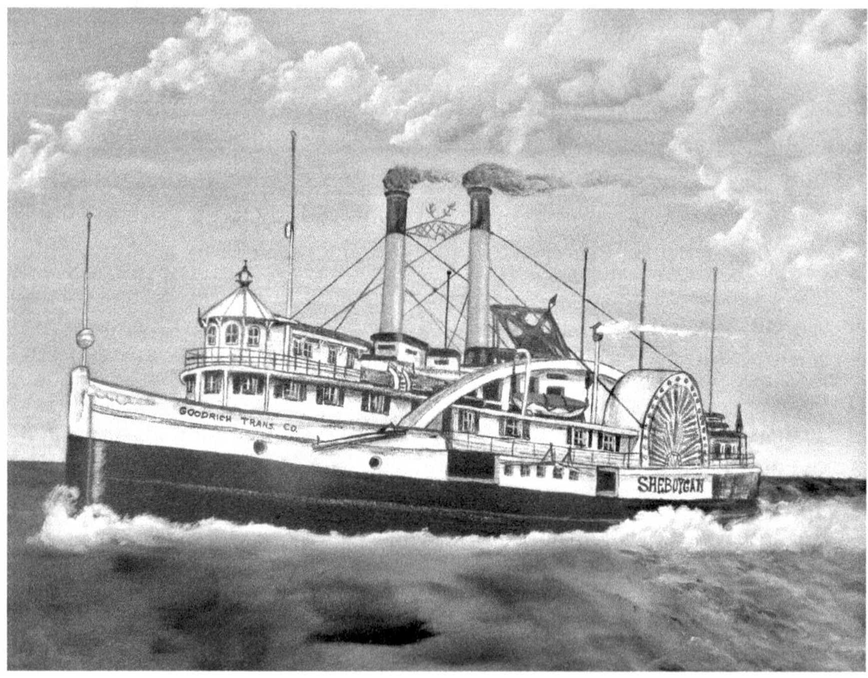

The second of four ships that carried the name Sheboygan. *Artwork by the author.*

passenger and freight vessel, the fourth a wooden harbor tug and the fifth a World War II frigate.

In 1886, the first baseball game was played in Sheboygan by an organized team named the Ellwell Boys. It took place on a vacant lot in the summer of that year. There were no seats, no admission was charged and nearly every man in Sheboygan attended the game.

According to official police records from 1888, Sheboygan Police made several arrests that year for idiocy. It makes one wonder how many arrests could be made today for the same offence.

In the 1890s, lake captains had little use for charts or compasses. To determine directions, they stepped out onto the deck on a sunny day and pointed the hour hand of their big gold watch at the sun. Then they located a spot halfway between the hour hand and twelve, and that was south. Try it—it works!

In the year 1895, the Sheboygan Light and Power Company was granted the right to operate electric streetcars in the city.

The year 1896 saw a resolution passed that ordered council proceedings to no longer be published in German and English; henceforth, they were to be published in English only.

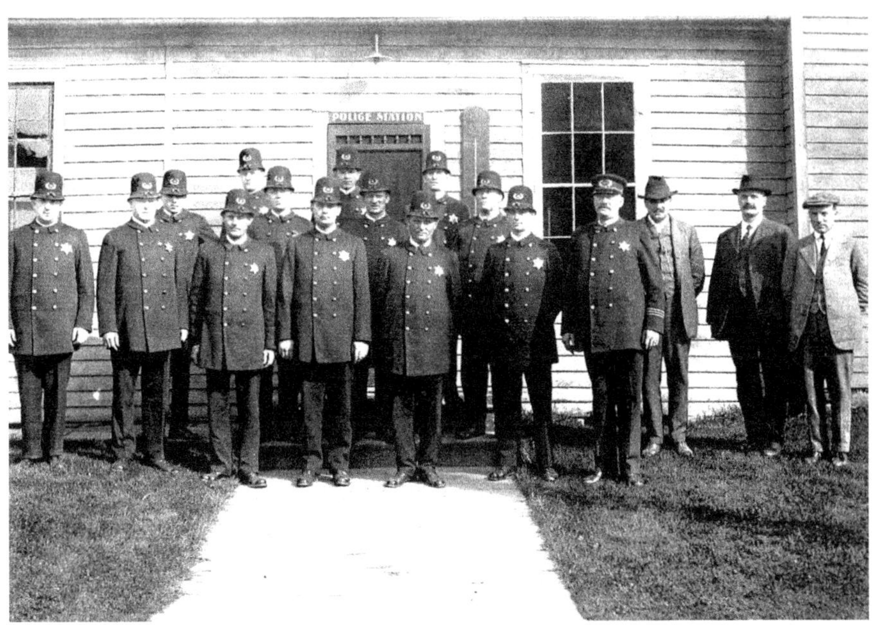

In 1888, the entire Sheboygan Police Department lined up for a group picture. *Author's collection.*

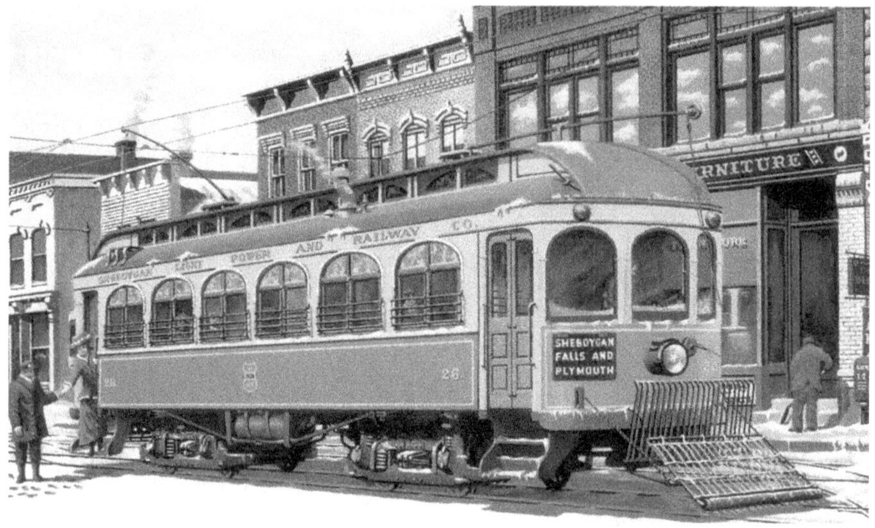

Car #26 at North Eighth and Pennsylvania Avenue. This car is still in existence and has been completely restored. *Courtesy Sheboygan County Historic Research Center.*

For many years, aldermen, bridge tenders and the cemetery sextants carried badges and had full arrest powers.

During the bicycle craze of the early 1900s, February 22 (Washington's birthday) was a very special day to bicyclers, for that was the traditional first day of the bicycle season. It was also the day the new models for the year came out, and bicyclers would line up early in the morning outside the bike shop to see them.

In the late 1890s and early 1900s, more furniture and wood products were manufactured in Sheboygan than any place on earth. It was reported that in 1888, 890,000 pieces of furniture were shipped out of Sheboygan.

At one time in Sheboygan, horse racing was extremely popular. During the summer months, North Sixth Street, which in those days was a dirt road, was often closed to traffic between Pennsylvania Avenue and Geele Avenue to permit horse racing.

The following item was taken from the February 15, 1906 edition of the local newspaper: "Nicholas Hoffman, who is 64 years old, bathed today for the first time in 50 years. He made a vow when he was 14 years old that he would never take another bath. A sheriff's deputy stood by while Hoffman was forced to break his vow."

In the year 1910, nearly ten thousand automobiles were sold in the United States, and predictions were made that the following year as many as twenty thousand would be sold. This figure was scoffed at by most people. It was just plain common sense to realize that the smelly, noisy automobiles would never replace horses.

During the winter months, when the roads were covered with snow, the City of Sheboygan would close city streets located on hills to accommodate children sled riding.

In 1912, the 1600 block of North Fifth Street was honored as the first concrete street in the city, and a small marker was erected. The street is now covered with asphalt; however, the marker is still there.

What may have been the world's first snowmobile was a strange-looking device that resembled an open car body with wooden skis on the front, propelled by a large screw at the rear and powered by a four-cylinder engine that was built by Falls Motors of Sheboygan Falls. Built for use in Alaska, it was known as the 1913 Burch Autosleigh.

The population of Wisconsin during World War I was so predominately German that it was feared that men drafted into the army would defect and go over to the German side once they arrived in Europe; not one ever did. Wisconsin units, in fact, fought with great bravery in World War I.

In the year 1919, the Sheboygan Merchants played the newly formed Green Bay Packers. The score: Green Bay 89, Merchants 0.

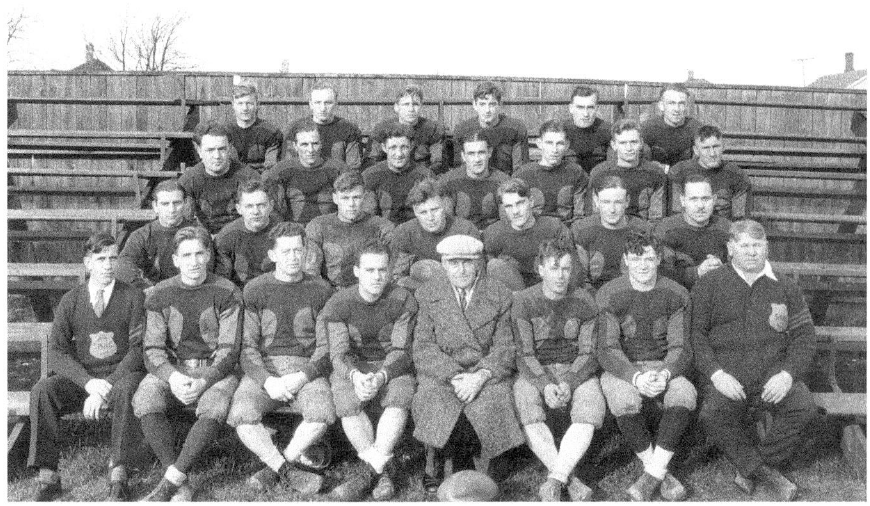

The Sheboygan Merchants Football team about 1919. *Courtesy Sheboygan County Historic Research Center.*

Many of the one-room schoolhouses had almost poetic names, such as the Bonnie View School and the Welcome School. And wouldn't it have been fun to go to the Starlight School?

In the year 1921, Wisconsin was the first state to pass a law eliminating all discrimination against women.

When the morning recess at a country school was over, the children would be summoned back to school by the teacher ringing a small handheld bell out the front door. Mischievous students at times would hide the bell so as to lengthen the recess period. This prank usually resulted in the child being severely scolded and sometimes enduring a trip to the woodshed.

By 1925, radio was becoming extremely popular, and it was about this time that "portable" radios began to appear. The first portables were huge contraptions with a large spider web–like antenna that had to be set up. Two heavy batteries, which weighed thirty pounds or more, were used to power these portables.

Police records from 1927 show that a young Sheboygan man who was arrested for "loafing on a public street" was found guilty and sentenced to jail for five days. One would hope the miscreant was not allowed to "loaf" while he served his sentence!

During the Roaring Twenties, Al Capone, the infamous Chicago gangster, was said to have passed through Sheboygan several times on his way to his north woods hideout. The main highway to northern Wisconsin in those days ran right down Eighth Street.

With Prohibition well underway an ad in the October 23, 1928 *Sheboygan Press* read, "188 proof alcohol, at only 59 cents a gallon can be purchased at the H.C. Prange Company."

In 1929, many homes in Sheboygan had a chicken coop in the backyard. Many instances of chickens being stolen were experienced. An alert police officer on foot patrol late one evening apprehended a culprit whom he caught in the act. The thief was taken into custody and hauled off to the police station. But the well-fed chicken thief was never charged, as he was a large, mixed-breed, black dog!

In the early days of Sheboygan radio station WHBL, one popular announcer, Tom Thomas, received what was then considered a large salary: the exorbitant sum of twelve dollars a week.

In October 1936, thieves broke into the warehouse of a local oil company and discovered that the company's safe had a small slot in the top through which money could be dropped without opening the door. The enterprising burglars bent the handle of a fly swatter in such a manner that they could

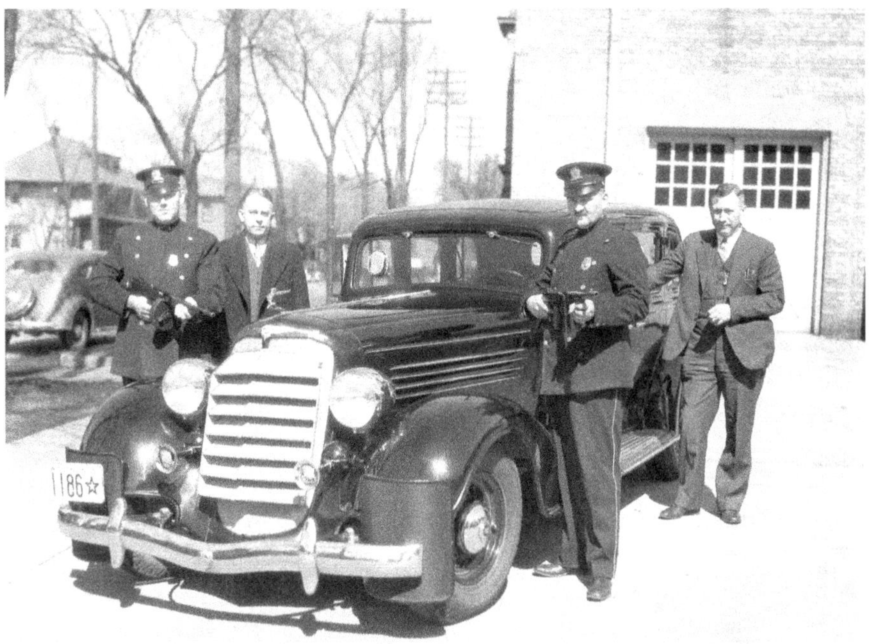

Armed with Tommy guns, Sheboygan police officers pose in front of the department's armored car, warning "criminals stay out of Sheboygan." *Author's collection.*

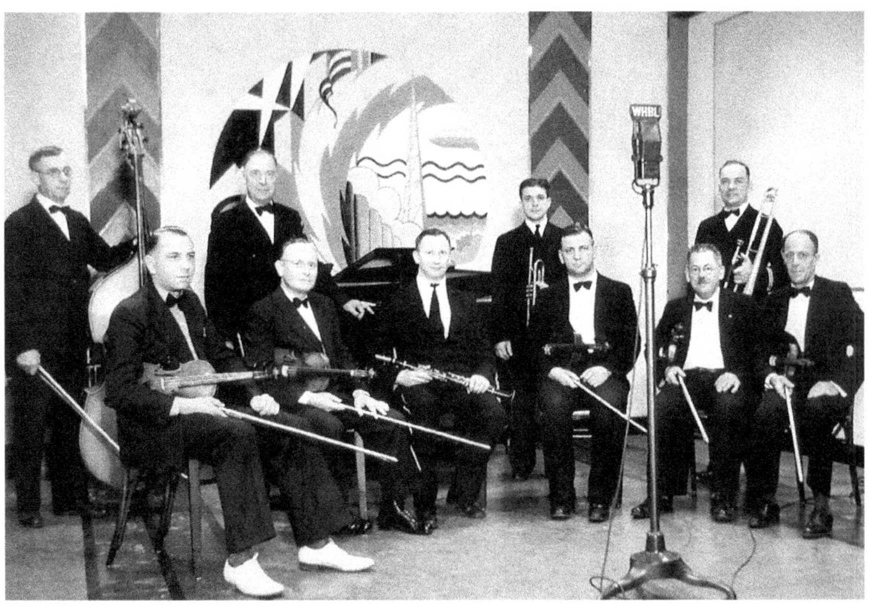

Radio Station WHBL's Concert Orchestra during the 1930s. *Courtesy Sheboygan County Historic Research Center.*

fish out over $510 (over $7,000 in today's money) out of the safe. To this day, the fly swatter–wielding bandits have never been caught.

On October 11, 1937, over five thousand people turned out to witness a flight of twelve military planes land at a field on the south side of Sheboygan. The mayor, aldermen and the Central High band all welcomed the fliers.

During the years of World War II, Sheboygan area industry turned out glider wings, shoes and boots, shell casings, brooms, clothing, canteens, mess kits and torpedo tubes for submarines. The Plymouth cheese factories manufactured cheese by the ton to feed hungry troops.

In 1956, there were twelve shoe repair shops in the city; today there are two. In many cases, shoes are a throwaway item, something that would never have been considered years ago.

The movie screen at the Star Dusk Theater was just over eighty feet high and fifty feet wide, making it one of the largest structures in the county.

In 1962, Wisconsin was the first state in the Union to require seat belts in all new cars sold in the state, beginning with the 1962 model year.

On Sunday mornings, radio station WHBL would broadcast the *Lutheran Hour*. In 1963, they decided to upgrade the station with new and more powerful equipment. Once the new equipment had been installed, the

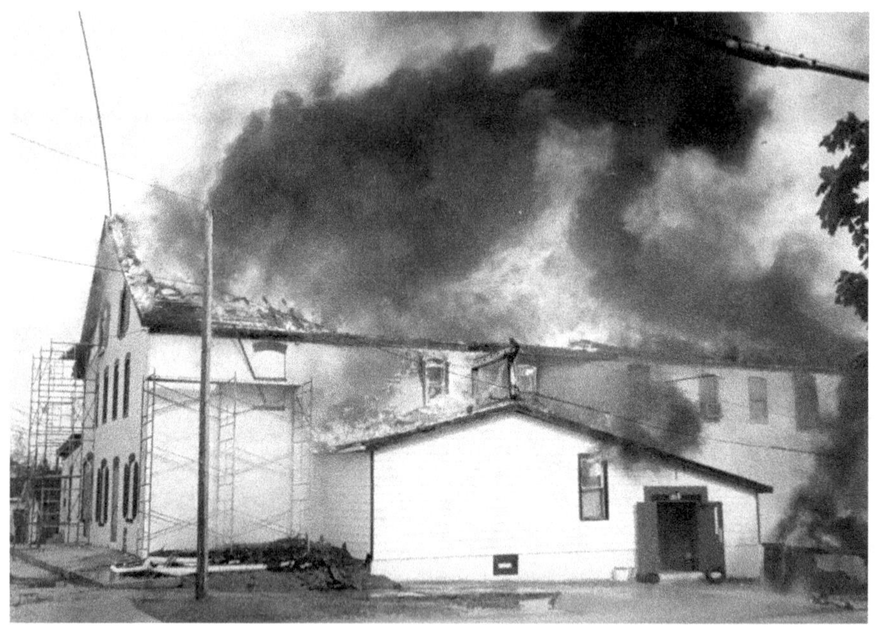

The 99 Hall fully engulfed in flames. *Courtesy Sheboygan County Historic Research Center.*

station engineer felt that a Sunday morning would be the best time to test it. On the morning of the test, the priest at Holy Name Catholic Church was in the pulpit about to start his sermon. The good father reached down, switched on the loudspeaker system and both he and his parishioners were startled to hear, "We now bring you the *Lutheran Hour.*" It seems that the new and more powerful equipment at the radio station had overpowered the church public address system. The bug was quickly repaired. The story was picked up by the national media and also reported by Paul Harvey and *Reader's Digest.*

On May 27, 1988, the 99 Hall was destroyed by fire. This building was the last remnant of Born's Park, a one-block-square entertainment complex that covered the area between Michigan Avenue to St. Clair Avenue and North Fourteenth and Fifteenth Streets.

Weather records indicate that only about 30 percent of our Christmases are white.

The Sheboygan Marsh, which for eons was a favorite camping and hunting ground of local Indians, covers over ten thousand acres.

The most often asked question I get is, "Where does the name Sheboygan come from?" There are several explanations; the one I favor is "where the waters meet"—in other words, where the Sheboygan River runs into the lake.

ABOUT THE AUTHOR

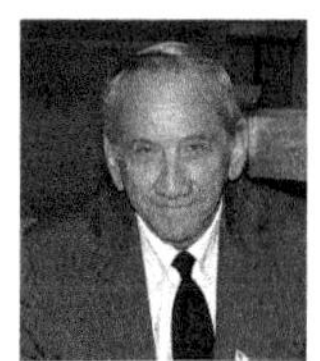

Bill Wangemann is a lifelong resident of Sheboygan, Wisconsin. From early on, he developed a strong interest in local history, especially the history of the Great Lakes. Bill is a twenty-eight-year veteran of the Sheboygan Police Department, where he served as a patrolman, emergency medical technician, crime scene photographer, police artist and crime scene reconstruction specialist. Bill is a board member of the Sheboygan County Historical Research Center in Sheboygan Falls and is also on the board of directors at the Sheboygan County Historical Society Museum. He is also a past member of the board of directors at the Mead Public Library. He has written three books that were published by the Research Center and has written over 360 columns on local history for various local newspapers. Bill also holds a seat on the Sheboygan Common Council as an alderman and has done so since 1999. In 1986, by act of the common council, Bill was appointed city historian, a position he still holds today. Bill is married and has three children, two stepchildren, eleven grandchildren, one great-grandson, three dogs and four cats. His hobbies are woodworking, model building, photography and drawing and painting.

www.ingramcontent.com/pod-product-compliance
Lightning Source LLC
LaVergne TN
LVHW010942100826
845153LV00002B/116

9781540205032